HEADLONG
INTO LIFE

Dedicated to all who suffer

HEADLONG INTO LIFE

Derek Lewis

Andy + Rachel

Enjoy with me

DGLP

Published by DGLP
3 Ceridwen Terrace,
Pontypridd,
Rhondda Cynon Taff,
CF37 4PD

ISBN 978-0-9565153-0-8
A CIP record for this title is available
from the British Library.

Cover design: Richard Lewis
Inner design and typesetting: Simon Hicks
Printed in the Czech Republic by Akcent Media Ltd

Contents

Beginnings

Life began at the centre of the world, my centre.

As is the case in every child, the realization of 'Self' becomes apparent, and the whole world rotates around your own consciousness. I found myself surrounded by aliens, all pushing and shoving me in every direction.

A Ponty boy was born, unaware of the joys, the struggles, the pains, and the sheer exuberance of the adventure ahead. The impermanence of life did not yet exist in my mind. As with the lotus flower, at the beginning, the muddy waters hide the beauty of the creation of a life, and this life, equally as precious as the next, must flower and enhance the world it has entered.

I look back at an ocean of experiences, then forward to the next flood of experiences that life has to offer. The images of India, Nepal, Pakistan, Yugoslavia, Berlin, Paris, Cardiff and many more, wash through my mind in such an overwhelming rush of emotion and pleasure, that I have to stop...

Now I must separate and concentrate on the incidents that changed me from a selfish individual into whatever I have now become. Earliest recollection. Aged two years, sitting on a table in Hayward's photographic studio in Ponty, rolling up my tie, and letting it drop... why do these superfluous memories stick in our minds?

The world was in free fall around us all in the early 40s, and yet the children of our time were oblivious to the pains being inflicted on our fellow man. Our consciousness could not yet comprehend situations not right there in front of us. We were the lucky ones, basking in the energy of play, strengthening our bodies and minds to face the future. An incident occurred at this time to illustrate our isolation from the naughty goings on in the world around us.

One evening in early 44, I was playing in front of our house with a toy wooden Tommy-gun, my one present joyfully received that Christmas. The sound of an aircraft, droning its way down the valley, was an obvious target for my very real new present. I proceeded to fire my prized gun at the target, letting out a resounding RAT-A-TAT-TAT-TAT of the all-wooden gun's ratchet mechanism. My memory tells me that the plane went into a screaming dive at this point, making me believe I had scored a direct hit and had succeeded in bringing it down. I remember only a fraction of a second after this as I was grabbed by the neck of my shirt and dragged under the stairs to safety.

I have to say that my two brothers never corroborated this story, but my memory of this incident is so strong, that I am sure it relates to a real event. To support this, it is recorded that a number of incidents occurred where German aircraft deliberately dropped their bombs on fields, away from many towns, so as not to harm anyone.

I am almost ashamed to admit to the following, but it must be said, and will, I am sure, give some amusement along the way. Age approx. four years, and very few pastimes other than those you created yourselves, and so knitting was an option not usually associated with the strong sex (tongue in cheek). It was a neighbour's daughter who was my tutor in this delicate art, and Molly taught me the physical skills to start a woollen wonder, but never gave me the knowledge to finish a project. For some totally unknown reason, I embarked on a pair of socks to begin my knitting career.

The main problem with this choice was the fact that one had to turn corners for the toes and heels, a skill I was sadly lacking, and so, having got started with the old re-cycled wool, donated by some knitting veteran, I threw myself into this new, and forgettable skill. Soon I was an expert, with the woollen wonder growing in length and with edges that were not straight. The mixture of colours, and the knots where I had joined each new colour, made the whole thing into a kaleidoscope of utter nonsense that looked more like the Dr Who scarf, not yet invented, but at least twice as long. It was my first and last attempt at this almost lost art, and I stuck to more suitable boy things like conkers and marbles from then on.

Here ends my limited memories of the conflict time, but my memory explodes into life on VE Day. The day was one of smiles and laughter, of sandwiches, of play, of running in all directions. An explosion of joy, not understood by myself, but welcomed as a new freedom to search for, and experience the Karma of the world.

Jelly, ah... that new taste to last a lifetime. The taste of a day that brings back a clear image of two garages on our road, transformed into a wonderland of vibrant colours, music, food, fancy dress and new hope. The tables in the road were a forest to run through and chase a future. This really was the start of an adventure to find Nirvana, that elusive goal that holds all hope and excitement.

This tiny world that comprised two streets, Mackintosh Road and The Avenue, was my whole world for a number of years, with narrow paths leading to school and my playground, 'the common'

My memories of Coedpenmaen Junior School are shallow. However, in future years, the school and its staff would become a source of inspiration to me, having influenced my thought processes, from selfish, to the now.

Golf, that infuriating game that tries the patience of the most placid person, raised its ugly head above the bunker's ridge. My two brothers, mum, dad, (but not the cat), were all totally hooked on this insular, selfish, and maddeningly fascinating pastime. Luckily for me I was not drawn into the addiction, but, being a strong family unit, I was led along a parallel path for some years. This was not without its benefits, as along the way we visited some amazing venues, including Southerndown and Royal Porthcawl, where I achieved the distinction of second place, in the under-fifteens. For this I received a watch... the best prize of the day.

But I digress. I feel it is important to try to show the importance here, of my family. Mum was a gentle, quiet and uncomplicated individual. She demanded little from life, other than life itself. She was totally caring of the family, but at a distance. She gave all three of us boys space to find ourselves, but at the same time made sure we had respect for everything around us. Mum was an international bridge player of some ability and is still remembered locally with great affection.

Mum's influence was not appreciated at the time, but in later life has shown itself to be of great value. She taught me more by her silent moments and her non-judgemental attitudes than all the every-day requests. One time in our lives highlights this to perfection. I had planned a trip around the world, hitch-hiking and working. At no time did she complain or discourage me, although I now realise she must have been frantic with worry, when I eventually left home on my travels.

Dad's quiet personality seemed to have little effect on my development. On reflection, the effect was subliminal. He was never forceful or vocal in his opinions, but one always felt he was at peace with himself. I think he may have been proud of my somewhat adventurous outlook on life, but never expressed this. He had been a wireless operator in the Merchant Navy during the First World War. The only action he saw was a close shave with a mine narrowly missing his ship in the Baltic. Ironically, it must have been close to an area I was to visit later.

Neither parents were demonstrative, nor affectionate in an outward way, but I believe the affection was always there, giving a warmth and a solidness to our relationship. My somewhat boisterous and flamboyant nature as a youngster was a reaction to my surroundings. One that I learned to adjust as I got older. My lack of awareness of my fellow man was to take many long years to adjust.

Bill and Bryan, my two older brothers, had totally different characters. Bill was private and introverted, silently working his way towards his own goals. Bryan was a flamboyant confident man, who knew exactly what he wanted. His ability to make friends would enable him to be successful at whatever path he chose. To illustrate this point, a story he often related to anyone who would listen, was when he worked for the pet food company Kit-e-Cat. He boasted it was good enough for human consumption. When some of his clients would disbelieve the claim, Bryan would open up a tin and eat. I cannot comment on the effects of these actions, but he was a very successful salesman.

Both my brothers eventually moved to South Africa to live, at the time of Apartheid. I was invited to join Bryan in SA in 1972 to take part in a project he was involved in, but that is for later in this journal. I shall tell you then who was in favour of racial segregation, and who was against.

To return to my early years in the two roads that were my world. 1947 – winter, snow, what a memory! Three or four weeks of snow so deep, the whole world seemed to stand still. Everyone in our street (and I am sure, in most others), dug channels from one house to another, criss-crossing the roads in lines of communication. How we managed to get food at this time I do not know, but at age seven, this really was not important. The hardships our parents encountered at such times were only appreciated much later on.

School and play took over our lives for some years. For me, play was the only important subject. I remember the occasional naughty prank, such as knocking on doors and hiding, more painfully, sneaking in to the allotments and gorging on gooseberries. I still feel the tummy pains when thinking about it. One action at this time that had a profound effect on my future, was when I borrowed one of my father's pipes and proceeded to smoke dried cabbage leaves under a rock on the common. My green face was never questioned by mum, but I am quite sure she had some idea of my stupidity.

The next few years saw horizons opening up before me, Barry Island, cinema and the YMCA Boys Club, where lifelong friendships were forged. Cinema, with its emphasis on heroics of the recent past and the emergence of colourful American spectaculars, made me believe I could, and would, become a star. Barry Island was to be the first sight of the Ocean, a sight that must have started the notions of travel, although it was after many visits that I began to wonder what was beyond the horizon. One memory in particular springs to mind, when I sat on the rocks at the end of the point, writing a song for my mum. While struggling with the tune in my head, trying to translate it into musical terms, I watched the tankers and freighters smoothly drifting towards their horizons, then disappearing by my next glance, as if by magic.

My father was a commercial traveller, selling machinery and general requirements for the South Wales farming community. He was one of the few to run a car in those times, This meant possibilities of trips out, not something today's youth would find unusual, but to us it was a passport to the big wide world. The most poignant trip was a one-hour journey to Barry Island or Porthcawl. The highlight of such outings was the first sight of the sea. This was greeted with howls of delight, usually by me, the feeling that has lasted a lifetime. I am sure that that experience had some influence on my desire to travel as much as I have. During these trips, I would often doze off, with the sound of the engine droning in my ears, and I would always swallow as the car changed gear. I was under the impression that the car was doing the same.

The Boys Club gave me the opportunity to take part in many stage productions, from pantomime to plays such as *Wind in the Willows*, where I played Toad of Toad Hall. A recent operation meant I was still in plaster on both legs, and the adjudicator in his deliberation made large of the way Toad had walked throughout the performance like a Toad. We did not inform him of the reasons, and sure enough, we won the prize for best play.

These plays and pantomime performances culminated in my being chosen to play the child part in a repertory company's show, in the local theatre. The Town Hall theatre was putting on a six-week set of plays by The Saville Players. I was told on the Wednesday evening to attend the theatre on Thursday to start rehearsals. To my

horror, I had just two days to learn the part before we started performances on the Sunday. Somehow, we got through the week, and
I was paid the princely sum of three guineas, this being the equivalent
of a week's wages for a man.

The female members of the cast were all supportive to me, moth-
ering me rather than treating me as a fellow thespian. However, some
of the male cast members took a somewhat different attitude. I felt
they treated me as a threat, as well as occasionally, seeming to take
too much interest in my welfare. Overall, the experience showed me
the backstage aspects of the acting profession, with the OTT histri-
onics, along with the strange terminology of their lingo, including
"sweetie" or "oh darling", making me feel exceedingly uncomfortable. I must make it clear here that there was no specific action that
prompted my decision to call a halt to my acting aspirations. Rather,
that the thought of living in the unreal world, pretending to be
someone else, was definitely not what I wanted in life.

This sudden realisation – a complete reversal of my intention to
make a career on the stage – meant that my young mind did not cope
too well with prospect of adjusting my plans. The walk home from
the theatre with my dad was very difficult. I was sure that I had found
my vocation in life, yet at the same time realised that I could not consider setting foot again on the stage. These opposites were
incomprehensible to me. My tantrums all the way home caused me
to get as close to a beating from my father as I would ever get.

Soon after, it became clear to me that the behaviour of the men in
particular was alien to my way of thinking. I vowed to make that my
last acting experience. I can see now that it was a watershed for me.
Until I started writing this book, it had not occurred to me that my
mindset was changed by an action or reaction to a particular event,
but this was the case.

I think the timing of these episodes came a couple of years before
the interest in girls became apparent. Luckily for me, it meant an
introduction to photography. I acquired my first camera, a Brownie
Flash B box camera. The chocolate colour of this object must have
been the reason for its purchase; the very camera now sits in a place
of honour amongst my memorabilia. This, without a doubt, had set
in stone the future I was to follow.

At twelve or thirteen I went on my first holiday, camping with the
local Boys Club. The destination eludes me; although I remember that
it was in the grounds of a private school, and some of the names are
still locked into the memory. Nick Jones was the club leader and his
assistant Max; two of the boys on the camp were Joey and Adrian,

both of whom have remained in the area. Few memories remain, except an early introduction to fishing by Adrian, and the non-stop smiling of Joey (not his real name). It was the practice at these camps to blanket bounce the boys to see who would go highest. Suffice to say I got that dubious honour. This would have been an honour worth remembering were it not for the fact that, on the last bounce, I remember quite distinctly flying way above the tops of the tents, only to land on my hip on a very hard floor: I had missed the blanket on the way down. A painful memory that only Joey may recollect, as he was about the same weight as me and also flew high in that practice.

There was one other excursion with the Boys Club the following year to Newton Abbot near Torquay, at a place I believe was called Churchill Field, a place I came across only a few years ago when re-visiting Barton Hall. Unknown to me at the time, they were only a mile apart. The field we camped in still looks the same, but I am sure the horse in the field can only be a distant relative of the one we used to try and ride.

Only three memories remain from this holiday, the walk to and from the pub and shop up the lane, the hot chocolate brewed each night in a large pot over an open fire, and the joys of the first and last real attempt at smoking fags. I well remember the one tent used for this purpose must have been the most unhealthy place on the planet each night, as the 'Turf' cigarettes were in abundance. I am quite sure this was a deterrent to my ever becoming an addict to the dreaded weed.

School Years
& First Job

School had rumbled along in a most uninspiring way, although there were a few interesting, if a little mischievous, occurrences. The earliest I can recall was the art room moment of genius. The art teacher was a character straight out of fiction. He was a chain smoking ex-deep-sea diver. Mr. Whitehead I recall never drew or painted anything, except maybe his living room walls, but would give very brief instructions, such as draw a fish, or someone's face. This, of course, was an open invitation to do exactly what we wanted, while he disappeared into his back room den to smoke another cigarette.

I decided to have a crack at a face and thought a profile would be the easiest option. I managed to complete what looked like a very bad likeness of the boy I had drawn. One of my mates in class saw my effort and took it to show Mr Whitehead, the smoker. He was delighted to see that Lewis [me] had captured a likeness of some note. Quite by accident, I had produced a very good portrait of King George V. If it had been in any way intentional I would have been proud of my work, but it was just about the only time I showed any talent for art. The drawing is probably in the Royal Collection now.

Very close to the art room was the assembly hall, where the school orchestra practiced and played. I was proficient enough to be included in the first violins, although there had been no audition for this lofty position. One day at rehearsal, we were practicing 'Overture to Berenice', when 'Cuce' Davies, the teacher, was called away. (Mr Davies as a child was allegedly very partial to cucumber.) I thought, what an opportunity to conduct this rabble. I took the baton, tapped the rostrum, and brought the boys in from the beginning. Several bars in the volume started to waver, and laughter echoed from some quarters of the orchestra, much to my disapproval. I became more and more flamboyant in my attempts to control the music, until finally, silence... Cuce was standing behind me and my embarrassment was somewhat obvious.

In assembly each morning we would scratch out hymns like taking your daily aspirin, and boredom often became the norm. This must have been the beginning of my interest in jazz, as I discovered the tune of 'Three Blind Mice' fitted beautifully into one of the hymns. Whether Cuce noticed or cared I will never know, but he never mentioned it.

And now, the one incident that I feel was out of character for me. To this day, I have no idea why I did it. I had a free period before break and went to the hall where ⅓ of a pint of milk would be given free to one and all as government policy to improve the diet of the nation's children. I must explain that milk and my body do not agree, so I wasn't intending to drink any of the stuff.

The hall was empty, and the milk was stacked and ready for the imminent race to partake of the abundant supply of the ghastly nectar. I proceded to carefully remove the silver foil top of one of the bottles, and emptied half a salt cellar into the milk. Then I replaced the silver top, gave the bottle a shake, and put it back in the crate. Confident that no one had seen my heinous crime, I took my position outside, where there was a clear view of the drama about to unfold. My big mistake was to invite some of my friends to witness the ensuing mayhem.

The result was greater than I could have imagined. A sixth former dutifully obliged by choosing my spiked bottle. He held it in his right hand with the silver top in his palm, turned the bottle upside down to unwittingly give the cocktail an extra stir, removed the top, and gleefully took a huge gulp of the glorious nectar. The ensuing mayhem does not have to be described in great detail, but the desired effect was magnificent. The response of my mates was uncontrolled laughter, and an obvious desire to vacate the area as quickly as possible. All would have ended well if the entire incident had not been followed by one of the sixth form prefects. His hand landed firmly on my shoulder, accompanied by the words, "Lewis, detention". My heart sank; the euphoria of the successful prank had made me careless in my peripheral observations. I realised I was not cut out to be a prankster or a thief, as it was clear I would leave too much evidence on display.

I was very fortunate not to be sent to the Head, as that would certainly have ended in a caning. Instead I was given three months detention, though I did not serve my full sentence, for reasons I will never know, though at the time, it caused some amusement in the sixth form study. I feel here, I must make an unreserved apology to the recipient of my misdemeanour, and trust he has learnt as much about forgiveness as I have.

I am sure it is obvious by now that my heart was not in school work. Although I was asked by Cuce to consider music and go on to University, I had already decided the path I was to take.

For some time I had forged a friendship with the proprietor of a local photographic firm, namely Ivor Alderson. He was a one-armed wedding and studio photograper whose character made a lasting impression on me. In April and May of 1956, during the build up to my 'O' level exams, my frequent visits to his shop in Taff Street bore fruit. I learnt that his assistant at the time was soon to finish to start a family, and sure enough, it was put to me one day, "would I be interested in training as his assistant?".

The offer of £2. 10s per week was too good to refuse. The results of my 'O' levels were now totally irrelevant. Although I managed a pass in mathematics and geography, my path was opening up before me, like emerging from a dark tunnel into bright sunlight.

Life at this time was a cocktail of new experiences. Gone was golf, gone was the stage experience, and gone was the wonderful child-hood, now relegated to memory. In came a feast of the new. Top of the list: learning my trade in all the aspects of my chosen profession. This world was of course black & white, and I quickly progressed through the technicalities of processing, lighting, composition and, most of all, man management, so important in wedding photography. I here have to admit that it took a lifetime to achieve any prowess in the last discipline. I am still learning.

Ivor was a great character, never complaining of disability, although at times it must have tested him to the limit. His prowess with one arm was quite extraordinary, markedly with his handling of cameras. I remember him lodging the camera on his left shoulder, using the stump of his left arm to steady the camera. He would focus with one finger, while holding the body of the camera in his palm.

It was not until some time later, that someone commented to me that I was taking a similar position when taking photographs. It has stuck with me to this day, and if one analyses this procedure, you will find it has a very practical function; it uses the body as a tripod. Try it yourself.

Ivor's sense of humour was one of his greatest assets, along with the patience he showed me during the time I spent in his charge.

Those who knew him may not agree with this statement, but I worked, and learnt from him for eighteen months. The darkrooms and work areas were under the shop, down a narrow, winding, wooden stairs. The film process room had the strongest smell of 'Hypo' I have ever encountered, and while loading spirals with film from the Saturday weddings, I would have time to reflect on my surroundings. The silence of this room seemed to echo the age of the building. Some 50 yards from the back window was a blacksmith, and yet I remember no sounds from there. What I do remember was the creaking of the floorboards of the shop above, there being no ceiling to the dark room.

At first, I would be somewhat apprehensive about spending too much time here, but a lesson I learnt was that we adapt to situations, and derive new skills from our experiences. Here, I have to relate one or two experiences which may contradict a previous statement. However, they were isolated incidents, and very rare. One day, I heard Ivor muttering and complaining in his printing darkroom. It continued for some time, on and off, but was getting more and more agitated. I entered the darkroom through the light trap, to find Ivor sat at his stool, by his enlarger, struggling to extricate a negative from its cellophane bag.

On this occasion I was in time to avoid papers and bags being hurled around the darkroom, but it seemed this was his Achilles heel. His fingers could not open the bag and extricate the negative. The fact that this was under the red light of the darkroom, and very cramped conditions, did not help. This brings me to an incident that occurred in the same area.

To explain the reason for the following, I must point out that the shop, upstairs, sold film, printing papers, chemicals, etc. Ivor would order his printing papers in boxes of 250. If the shop had no supply of papers in the quantities the customer wanted, Ivor would count out papers from his box and pack them for the customer. On the day in question, we were both printing in the darkroom when the call came from the shop, over the intercom (a very modern gadget for the day), for 50 post-card printing papers. Ivor proceeded to count out the papers, slowly walking towards the exit, as I continued printing. When I emerged from the darkroom, I was somewhat bemused to see Ivor still counting out the papers by the window. Anyone who remembers black & white printing will know that these papers were light sensitive, and are ruined if exposed to light. On realising his mistake, he lost it, hurling the papers in all directions. The shower of now ruined papers littered the outer work-room, but annoyance soon turned to laughter, and another memory was cemented into the brain.

He introduced me to his musical tastes, many of which have remained with me. However it was my mother that set me on a road to the classics, when we went together to the New Theatre in Cardiff to see Wagner's opera, *Tannhäuser*. The overture instantaneously registered a lifelong path into the great music of our world. At first, it was only classical and trad. jazz, that filled my musical tastes. That was to change.

For now, I went on a relentless selfish path of learning and self-indulgence. I could only see the narrow path in front of me, ignoring the effects that my actions had on others, especially my family. I recall a plethora of films at the time glorifying war and heroism and, being an avid film-goer, I remember having some strange delusions of grandeur. I am quite sure that this exposure led me to search for adventure and travel, but, again, gave me a false notion of superiority. I have for many years now been very ashamed of my attitude towards others, especially when I travelled to India.

It was around this time that the game of tennis inexplicably was linked to a healthy interest in the fairer sex. I have to admit that tennis was never a great passion of mine, but I have always maintained the other interest. I am sure all readers do not need to be reminded of the passions that burn in those first encounters, and so I leave it to your imaginations.

Important as these milestones are, they are not really important in the context of what I am trying to convey. What is important to me now had not even entered my head at that time. My total respect for my fellow man is only now taking a real hold in my 'consciousness', and it would take much heartache, and pain, not just to myself, to even start on the journey towards an understanding of 'Self'.

Time to return to the mundane happenings that filled my days. I had, by this time, forged friendships that still stand firm today, with the local Italian community prominent in this. In particular, Marenghi and Bertorelli were café owners in the town, and proved to be amongst my closest friends. In addition to these, I cannot overlook the early influence of the girlfriends, although I would not dare to presume that any of my friendships at this time, would even be remembered by them.

After a trip to the cinema, J. and I ran to catch the bus, boarding the double-decker. J. proceeded to the upper deck (no driver to bother us up there) but on the way up her shoe fell off, rolled down the stairs, and off the bus. As any gallant suitor would, I tried to stop the bus, but the conductor refused. And so, with no thought for the consequences, I held on to the bars on the rear platform, leaned back, and thought of England (sorry, Wales) and dropped onto the silky tarmac of the Broadway. It must have looked like the Keystone Cops film; my legs running like demented pistons, until eventually, and inevitably, I dived headlong along the tarmac, grinding to a stop with now skinless hands, knees but not bumpsadaisy.

The bus continued, with a worried looking J. peering after me, and I caught the next bus, eager to deliver the lost shoe to J. some two stops along. I arrived at her home bloodied, holding the offending shoe, to be greeted with somewhat frantic mum. "What have you done with my daughter" I had fully expected to be greeted like a soldier returning from the trenches, instead it seemed I was about to be accused of abduction or a similar heinous crime.

All was well eventually when J. arrived home, shoeless. With touching concern, she had doubled back to find her injured partner, only to find no trace. I got an extra kiss and cuddle that evening. Ah, good memories.

At this time I attended many different denominations of the local churches, sometimes for months at a stretch. All of these churches would insist on their own righteousness, without respect, it seemed, to others. One by one I moved on, sometimes, in a controversial way. While attending a local Catholic service with my girlfriend and her parents, the priest began his sermon, and proceeded, in my opinion, to contradict himself, and show an insular disregard for any that were not inside the church's clutches. I stood and quietly removed myself from the church. Suffice it to say, it was the end of that affair, but it is significant to me, that this, and other similar incidents eventually led me to reject Christianity.

The hectic life in the photographic world was punctuated every Saturday with a conveyer belt of 16 to 20 year olds tying the knot. It was usual back then to time your wedding to get the maximum tax relief, by marrying just before the end of tax half-year. March and September were the dreaded dates, so it became the norm to marry on the Saturday before the deadline. One such day, I was given two weddings in the morning. The first was in Ynysybwl, a couple of miles from my home town. I only took photographs at the chapel, leaving the shots of the reception to Ivor later. The time between this and the next ceremony, back in Ponty, was very short. With my case with the cameras in, and no bus available, I started back the two or three miles. There was a short-cut over the mountain, and I was confident I would make it in time. I know what you are thinking now, reader, but no, I did make it, albeit in a very sweaty state. What I do remember about these times, was that the huge pressure to succeed gave me a good grounding in control of 'Self'.

On another occasion, I was sent to do a wedding about half a mile from the shop, at St. Mathews. It was another of those hectic days, the boss at his weddings elsewhere. I had been given two cameras in my brown leather case and off I went. I was early and set up the main camera confident of a successful shoot. The camera jammed. No problem I thought, and loaded the second camera. Oh no! Nothing working.

By now the bride's arrival was imminent, so I told a member of the wedding party I would return as swiftly as possible. It was another run back to the shop, and, after a quick explanation, two new cameras were taken from the window display, and I was on my way back to eventually complete a successful wedding.

All these experiences at the time seemed only stressful and annoying. On reflection, I am sure they helped me to understand myself. These and many more long forgotten incidents gave me confidence to move on to other challenges. It was around now that I started to get itchy feet. The travel bug began to nibble away at my subconscious.

I had fallen for a wonderful young lady from Church Village. I can vividly remember the conflict with myself over Travel and Work. Shouls I continue in the local job? It was normal for us to arrive back at her home, talk, laugh and inevitably miss the last bus home. Those long walks home were full of thought and heartache, and when I made the inevitable decision to move on, Pat's final words still make me wonder 'what if?'. They were "I won't be here when you come back". I regrettably lost touch from that day to this.

The die was cast early in February 1958. An advert appeared in a local newspaper for a press photographer on a holiday camp in North Wales. I sent off an application. Not content to sit and wait, I asked Ivor for time off to go and make a personal appearance to show how keen I was. Thursday was half-day closing in Pontypridd, so some weeks later, I caught a train at around midnight, and spent a sleepless night making my way to Pwllheli, through the magnificent scenery of mid and North Wales.

I arrived at around 7.30am. And could not wait to find the home of Mr Chapman, the photographic manager. Turning up at his door, bleary eyed and hungry, I rang the bell and waited. Eventually, a very tired looking gentleman appeared at the door, quizzically peering at this unwelcome early arrival. I introduced myself, and the immediate reply should not really be written down here. He then suggested I go get something to eat and return in an hour or so.

I returned to find Mr Don Chapman somewhat refreshed and ready to hear my story. I told him I had wanted to speak directly to him rather than telephone and try to show him that the experience I already had would qualify me for the job. He explained that he only took on experienced press photographers as a rule, and asked one or two very quick questions. After a short silence he said, "because you have shown such enthusiasm and travelled all night just to show how much you want the job, you start in three weeks, a week early to learn the ropes".

Two stories related to me much later by Pete Wilson give an insight into Don Chapman's character. Don returned to his office one day to find a visitor waiting for him. Suddenly remembering he had an interview that morning and assuming this was the interviewee, he proceeded to explain the requirements of the post. He explained a knowledge of cameras and flash-guns, as well as black & white printing, would be an advantage. Well, he continued, are you interested in the job? Somewhat confused, the visitor said he would consider the offer, but asked if he would mind paying the bill for the milk first – he was the milkman!

On another occasion, Don had a call from a colleague in one of the other camps to say they were out of a certain size of photo printing paper. As the matter was quite urgent, and posting was not a suitable option, they agreed to meet half way in an hour. Don put the stock of paper in his car and set off to meet his counterpart from the other camp. They duly met at the prearranged pub and, not having seen each other for a while, stayed a while to catch up on events, eat and have a beer. Soon they realised they should get back to their respective camps, and set off. When Don arrived back at camp the paper was still on his back seat.

As I returned home after my visit, Don's words showed me in practical terms, that if you want something badly enough, go and get it. Ivor was the consummate gentleman and actually helped me in my preparation for my new challenge. I owe a huge dept of gratitude to his friendship and professionalism. The lessons he taught were invaluable and still as relevant today as they were then.

By this time I had acquired my own cameras, both cine and medium-format. My pride and joy was the Panta camera bought from Ivor before moving on. I sold the camera some time after and never imagined I would see it again. Many years later I met the guy I sold it to. Although it no longer worked, I bought it back off him and it is a prized part of my camera collection. It was even restored to full function by my son Donald some years later still. That remains one of the best Christmas presents ever.

The excitement of the new challenge helped in blocking out the loss of Pat, but so many new friends were appearing every day, and the pace of life in a holiday camp left no time for reflection. One shocking incident working on camp happened when I was in the ball-room, taking photographs of contestants in a competition. I turned the camera to wind on to the next exposure and the glass front of my flashgun fell out and smashed on the floor. At the same moment I had instinctively put my hand to catch the glass. Unfortunately for me I was too late, and my little finger of my left hand short-circuited the flash-gun. I got a considerable shock and ended up on the floor, quivering like a jelly. Not that I can remember much about it. I was whisked to the medical room, but released very quickly to return to the job I had just left, getting a huge, but embarrassing ovation. Later, the doctor informed me that my heart must be in good condition as such a shock could easily have killed me. So went my first cat-life.

The whole season was a resounding success, with the camp press sales record broken several times during the season. I purchased my first motorised transport, namely, a Barini 50cc moped with two gears, slow and slower. Towards the end of the season, I decided to make a trip home, leaving Friday evening, to get back by Sunday 9.30am. That Friday evening was hot and humid, with the inevitable increase in the flies and midges to keep me company all the way home. I was not particularly hungry when I arrived, as I had con-sumed a copious number of the aforesaid, leaving my appetite somewhat subdued.

I felt very proud of myself when enjoying the homecoming with the family, boasting of my weekly wage; which was at least double that of my dad. On reflection, I am not sure if this made my parents happy or sad. When the season ended soon after, I was brought down to earth with a bump. Being unemployed in a recession is not easy, but there is always a challenge to be found, and so I had a go at self-employed handyman.

I set about advertising in shop windows and telling as many people as possible of my new venture. After a little burst of painting jobs, I started to expand into glazing, gardening, clearing sites and much more. It meant having to report to the unemployment exchange was a lot easier. I just had to report I had earned enough to live on and they left me alone. I am sorry to say that I did drop one large clanger. While painting at one of my first jobs, I decided to shake a tin of paint, fumbled and dropped it, spilling a large amount of paint on the lady's carpet. I cannot remember how I solved the problem, but I do remember that the lady in question was very understanding. It has always remained in my memory as a good example of a calm and non-judgemental attitude. I do not mean that I ignored this situation, I made restitution fully, but it showed me that taking a belligerent attitude to some situations is not the best way to solve the problem.

During this period, I had been in communication with Barry, a guy I had met in Butlins. We had discussed the possibility of getting a contract to take photographs on a caravan site in Leysdown, on the Isle of Sheppey in Kent. With my knowledge of printing and the technical side, and his confident salesman prowess, we would make a good team. And so we agreed to start operations in April of that year.

Berlin

Before I start my holiday-camp story, I must relate a pivotal decision made at this time. I had been restoring a BSA C.12 motorcycle, fitting a new engine which needed running in. I was assured that I should ride at around 30mph for a couple of hundred miles, then 35mph and so on until I had done around 2,000 miles. I felt that pottering around locally would be somewhat arduous, so decided on a longer trip.

After the war, Berlin had become a focal point for much of the tensions of the day. It seemed a good way to start my travel adventures, killing two birds with one stone, running in my motorcycle and exercising my wanderlust.

And so, with a week or two before the summer season's start, I donned my gear, and set off with an excitement in my gut that I could taste. I was so proud of my magnificent machine, with its dark red fairing protecting me to some extent, but the speed of travel was sadly curtailed by the running-in process. I apologise to all those delayed by my slow speeds at this time. This knowledge to this day reminds me that none of us know exactly the reasons for other peoples actions. A little understanding can go a long way.

The journey was reasonably uneventful until reaching somewhere in the Rhine Valley, where I had been so taken with the glorious scenery that I took my eyes off the road for just a moment, and bang! At first I thought something on the bike had broken, but no, I had run over a road sign, warning drivers of road-works. Embarrassed, I rode on, heart pounding, having learnt another lesson.

Nights were generally spent sleeping alongside the bike, using public facilities to wash and brush up. On reflection, I do not think I was in a fit state to attempt fraternising with the girls. This was not at the forefront of my mind. My goal was getting ever closer. I had been warned that approaching the 'Berlin Corridor' from West

Germany to Berlin had certain restriction to follow. It was a fair distance, some 90km. You had a restricted time to make the journey. If you failed to show at the checkpoint within the allotted time, East German police would find you and arrest you. You were not allowed to leave the confines of the road, but there was one lay-by to rest. I stopped here for a break, and it proved to be hugely beneficial to my progress. I got chatting to a lady driver while here, commenting on the activity of the East German military on manoeuvres alongside the road. All this, I remember, was simply exciting, and there was no fear at all. I was totally innocent of the seriousness of the whole situation, and consequently did not take too much notice of protocol in these situations.

The lady in question however, had good knowledge of this situation, and strongly advised me to be very careful on the approach to West Berlin. It seems that the road signs could easily be misread, and you would end up in East Berlin, where you would spend two or three days in custody, and would have to pay a fine to get released. Luckily I did not put this to the test, as I followed behind her into West Berlin. Thank you lady, whoever and wherever you are.

Berlin: what a city. Vast, divided, vibrant and exciting. The populous, living in fear that they may have to leave at a moment's notice, were often packed ready for the possibility. Yet, life went on at some pace, with bars and cafés the places to sit and ponder. Although I remember the feelings I had in this situation, I have absolutely no recollection of where I stayed or ate, yet the memory of VWs driving recklessly on the wide roads of West Berlin is prominent in my memory, including some minor accidents occurring it seemed, in slow motion, with the occupants taking a cursory glance at the minor damage and moving on. I have no idea why these incidents are remembered or mentioned here but I often think of these mundane experiences, so there must be a reason.

Checkpoint Charlie. The romance and the poignancy of this location, with its place in the history of Berlin, was in its infancy. The daily dramas of life were to be experienced here. East Berlin, an enigma for me just a stone's throw across the Wall, invited me and all except West Berliners to visit. I am sure I do not have to explain to too many readers the details of the situation in this divided city at this point in history, but it must be understood that the delicacy and brutality of the actions of both sides, is not for me to comment on, merely to tell as I saw at the time.

I approached Checkpoint Charlie on my gleaming motorcycle, with the then modern fairing, and checked in at the West Office manned by the Americans. "Good morning sir," in a broad U.S. accent, "how long are you intending to stay in the East, sir?" I replied I had no idea, but enough time to look around. "If you are not back with us by around 3.00pm, we will send in a patrol to find you." My naivety made me simply smile, but said OK to appease the guy, and rode through the zigzag of no man's land to the East guards. My feelings then were very strong and superior, almost showing off my freedom to one and all. I have to say that those feelings now make me ashamed.

I was confronted with the desolation of Stalin Strasse, a street of shells of buildings, still in the state they must have been at the end of the War. Still, it was all just so exciting to be seeing first hand the places where so much history had so recently taken place, and I could not wait to meet the people of this strange landscape. I found an area to park the bike near some shops and entered one selling vinyl records, where I soon got chatting to a member of staff. His English was marginally better than my German and I eventually bought a ten inch LP of Chopin's Piano Concertos by the Prague Philharmonic, still somewhere in my collection.

Suddenly the salesman stopped talking to me and quickly moved away, much to my dismay. Some moments later he spoke to me and explained that we had been watched by secret police and he was fearful of his safety. All this now seems surreal, but it really did happen and made me begin to see the reality of the world around me. Soon though reality would be brought home in no uncertain manner. I remember I had to be careful to have changed my West German Marks into East German Marks at one of their banks, as the black market value of the Mark was ten times more. If you had no proof of where you had changed the money used to purchase goods, you could be arrested and jailed. I had managed to avoid these banana skins and continued my sightseeing, meeting an American visitor when I returned to my bike.

He had joined a group of locals that had gathered to look at my bike, marvelling at its sleek lines. It took a little time to extricate myself from the admiring locals, and the American and I decided to do some exploring. We eventually left the bike and went on foot wandering into interesting areas. What we did not know at this time was that we were close to the Wall, on the wrong side.

There were few people around and it became obvious only much later, with hindsight, that there was a good reason. We were oblivious and continued our exploring eventually finding ourselves near some old barbed-wire. I peered over to sight a gun boat on the canal. I called my fellow visitor to look at my discovery. What happened next has probably been told by my compatriot, somewhere in America, as many times as my version.

On looking back from our discovery, I saw, in slow motion, an East German guard leaving a trench, pushing his helmet back on his head, pulling his strap under his chin, taking his sub-machine-gun off his shoulder, pulling back the cocking hammer, and pointing the gun at us. We froze, and I shouted in very bad German "Nick spraken, English". He must have been a softy, as he did not fire. He did however tell us to leave the area in very colourful German, none of which we understood exactly, but got the message. My second cat-life, gone.

My recollections of the perception of the situation was one of exhilaration at being a part of the history that unfolded around me, blissfully unaware of the actual pain of the intolerance and violence imparted to the unfortunates in its midst. My feelings, now, are fearful of repetition in our society of a similar intolerance towards our fellow man, with anger, intolerance and a lack of respect for ourselves, let alone others.

Looking back now at the incredible memory, and realising that in the time I was there, several East Germans were killed trying to escape, as was to happen for years after the Wall had been built, I realise my good fortune. Perhaps my naivety was my salvation. I do have a souvenir of this visit, as I still have somewhere, a piece of the Wall, the importance of which now seems irrelevant, as the memory itself is the souvenir.

The journey home was uneventful, but pleasant, and included a visit to Beethoven's birthplace. Travel had taken hold of me, being foremost in my thoughts for the next few years.

Let me here relate a pleasant excursion made around this time to London with Derick, a long time friend for whom I would later be Best Man. We met up with my cousin Peter, then living in the Cromwell Road area, to do a little sight-seeing as well as take in a concert. The usual round of photo and cine film shots were out of the way, before attending a concert at the Royal Festival Hall, where we were to see an all Beethoven program, conducted by the great man himself, Otto Klemperer. This now frail old man was helped to the rostrum by two aides, then sat at a stool to lead the Philharmonia. A most unforgettable night of music. Regrettably, this was one of his last public performances, with all three of us honoured to have heard the great man in that wonderful setting, the memory of which remains with us.

Time to take on a new challenge using the knowledge already gained to eke out a living working for oneself. Barry and I arrived in Kent for the summer season at the caravan park, to try to scrape a living taking and selling photographs to the holiday-makers. My partner in this venture was Barry Smith, alias Alistair Barrington Smyth, this name clearly highlighting his character, the contrast between us forging a good friendship as well as a successful business partnership.

We arrived at Leysdown some two weeks before the punters to set up the darkroom and confirm the details of the contracts with the several camp clubs. We had been given an old caravan to stay in by one of the camp owners, Mr Frank Purvis. Basic is the only way to describe it, but the excitement of life relegated this mild inconvenience to insignificance.

The shed which had become our darkroom was a mile or so from the camps, so my motorcycle stood us in good stead, ferrying ourselves and bits and pieces to and fro. As I write these words, I have a visual memory of the streets, shop, pub, sandy verges and most of all the feelings in my head that were there at the time. I cannot describe the pleasant and yet eerie experience this is having on me right now, but I am sure there must be more and more of these feelings hidden just below the surface. It is just a thought, that the actual writing down of incidents could have similar effects on anyone: try it.

The first weeks were tough. No money and lots of hours building and setting up the darkroom. At last, the punters started to arrive, very few at first, so hunger was very real. I remember the first Friday night very well. We had taken some photos that week, but our sales were non-existent, so we decided, just before the club closed, that we would try our hand at busking. I got my violin out and stood outside the exit to the club. I have to admit here, that my prowess with the fiddle was somewhat limited. I now believe that the few shillings we made that evening was either sympathy or a desire to shut me up. I seem to remember the three tunes I played, were 'Over the Sea to Skye' 'I'll take you home again Kathleen' and some short excerpts from Beethoven's 'Violin Concerto'.

The fish and chips from the local chipy tasted that little bit sweeter that night, and it became a regular haunt for us all season. Luckily, it did not become necessary to do any more busking, although the owner of the club had heard me sing some songs, and asked me to repeat them on the little stage. It soon became a requisite of our photo tenancy to sing most nights. My repertoire was very limited, and I remember I wrote a couple of extra verses for a little variation. The following is a small sample:

Oh dear, what can the matter be,
Three old ladies got locked in the lavatory,
They were there from Monday till Saturday,
Nobody knew they were there.

The first one's name was dear Mrs Humphrey,
She went in there and sat down so comfy,
But then she found she couldn't get her bum free,
And nobody knew she was there.

And on and on. I remember there was a keyboard player and drums, and I must here apologise to them, for the trauma it must have caused. The other verses I shall leave to your imagination, but at the time they did raise a few eyebrows. I did one other song, 'The Wolf Cub Song', again very silly, but seemed to help our sales of photographs.

Here I must make another apology to a certain Miss Violet Heales. She was a visitor to one of the camp-sites and we often chatted while I worked, but no more than that. On reflection, I realise I was some-what insensitive at the time and being so engrossed in the business, paid little attention to her. I do remember visiting her at her home in South London on the sixth or seventh floor of a high rise. From that day to this we have had no contact. I trust, Violet, you have had a happy life. I remember you with some affection.

At this same time I had a once-in-a-lifetime experience. Whilst sheltering from an electric storm in a loft adjacent to the local pub, luckily with doors open, a thunder ball shot past, around, and back out, leaving the few of us there dumbstruck. Maybe these moments were the catalyst for the adventures brewing in my head, although at the time, nothing specific had taken shape.

Barry acquired a car. We both drove regularly so I decided I ought to get a licence. The practice I had had, served me in good stead, as, with only one or two lessons, I went for my test in Canterbury. I remember driving there with a compatriot in Barry's Morris Traveller, and just before the test, one of the spark-plugs literally stopped firing. We called in to a local garage, explained the situation, and to our great relief, changed the plug. I passed my test at the first attempt.

This meant I would now have to get my own wheels. Everything had to be NOW. No "let's wait a while," oh no, straight to a very small local garage to see what they had that I could afford. Not much I have to admit, but, with a little persuasion and a little deposit, I acquired a 1934 Morris Minor, with a windscreen wiper worked mainly by hand, a front windscreen that opened, a running board on each side to ride on and a braking system that required considerable effort and distance to come to a stop. The clutch was on the left, the accelerator in the middle and the brake (ha ha) on the right. I remember that while braking, there was a considerable pull to the left, somehow not too important to worry about. Today it simply would have had to be scrapped.

I named the car 'TIZA BUGA' and painted this on the front of the car, along with many more silly things all around the bodywork, trying to distract from the considerable rust. At the end of the season, the first and last at Leysdown, I returned via London, home to Wales with a burning for life's experiences to continue at pace. The next adventure was to be prompted by my rejection for the Royal Navy, because of my high-arched feet.

Unemployed, and bored, I decided to try to get a job in the Merchant Navy. Not so easy. To get a seaman's card you had to have a job, to get a job you had to have a card. I knew there must be a way, so I travelled to Harwich (Parkeston Quay) and made enquiries as to how to get around this. I did, and spent the next four months travelling back and forth to The Hook Of Holland.

We were ferrying troops back and fore to Europe, in an ex-German navy vessel that had been scuppered by its captain at the end of the war in 1945. It was reputed that he had hung himself in the forward section of the ship, and, of course, his ghost was sup-posedly haunting that section. I got the job of general dogsbody as there was a shortage of men wanting this rather temporary post. My duties were mainly as a fire clock watch, which meant touring the extremities of the vessel, and turning a key at set points, thus main-taining safety on board. It meant, of course, wandering the very area where the late captain lurked, and when we had no troops on board, it could be a little scary to say the least.

When the troops were on board with us, it was a completely dif-ferent story. The noise and the chatter was incessant, and there was never a dull moment. Never was this more poignantly obvious than one trip to The Hook of Holland. The ten hour crossing was around half way, when a fearful storm blew up. It reached force ten (storm). I was not on duty at the time, so could enjoy, or otherwise, the thrill of the occasion if I so desired. I went out on deck to witness one of the most amazing sights I have ever seen. We were a very small vessel, only a few thousand tons, and could be described as a cork being tossed around in a white water rapid. When we reached the crest of a wave you looked down into a valley of water, and conversely, when reaching the floor of the wave one looked up at a mountain.

This was the only occasion that I was sea sick, but even this could not dampen the joy of the situation, and the lasting memory of wondrous pleasure. On reflection, not having a safety harness on probably put me in some danger, but that thought never entered my head. I do not count this as another cat-life lost. I have to confess to a minor misdemeanour. On a similar trip, and a rough sea, I was on my round of fire watch and approached the forward deck to clock in. The troops were all in or around their bunks and the sight and smell hit me like a sledge-hammer. The chain reaction of one being sick prompted a situation to be avoided, and I did. Sorry lads, but I could do nothing to assist in that situation, but I am quite sure you all survived.

In addition to my watch duties, I assisted in the galley and learnt the basics of cooking. I became a master of the toast and tea, with a second master in coffee brewing. I had not yet become a drinker of any hot beverages, but must have started the process at this juncture. One early morning, I prepared trays of breakfast for the officers and was to deliver same, below, to their quarters. I must here explain what is common knowledge to all seamen. When at sea, and going below or aloft, one should be aware of the ships motion. If one times the ascent or descent correctly, you are assisted by the up and down motion of the vessel. If, however, you do the opposite, you will find the equal and opposite applies. If you are carrying trays of tea, coffee, toast and lots of breakables, well, I need not explain.

The resounding crash should have woken the dead, but no reaction at all. Perhaps the odd tipple the night before had deepened the sleep. Another lesson learnt.

This short interlude in my career gave me an appreciation of some situations that would never have occurred to me had I not tasted them for myself. It also started my long affair with cigars. It was undoubtedly the glorious smell of the dreaded leaf that was to draw me into its dreaded clutches. Luckily for me, I never inhaled the smoke and this proved to be a lifesaver to me in later life. DON'T.

London

Hitch-hiking had become a norm for me by now, and many a chat with friendly drivers gave me an appreciation of the predicaments of others, and, I think, began the process of understanding myself. I wanted to experience as much of life as was possible, and this desire still burns inside. I still remember the excitement of every excursion I made to the continent, sometimes just for a day or two. I usually went alone as I was so impulsive. It was often impossible for my friends to organise themselves in time.

London had always been a future target for experience for me, and the time was right for this adventure to begin. I had, some years earlier, been involved in a race to hitch-hike to the Monument in London organised by a few of my school friends. We set a limit of cash to be used, enough to get home afterwards, and the first team to lower the Welsh flag over the parapet of the Monument would be declared the winner. I have absolutely no recollection of any more details of this venture, and so it must remain an enigma.

I had now decided that London would have the pleasure of my company, and simply donned my rucksack, and left for the Smoke. Swiftly getting a temporary job with an advertising agency as a printer, I found a bed-sit, and began to discover the delights of the city. Classical music was the big draw, and it was in abundance wherever I went. It was closely followed by a fascination with traditional jazz, which had a large following by then.

I progressed to a photographic salesman with a large chain outlet, but my honesty in advising customers to only buy the equipment they needed soon got me dismissed for not selling enough of the higher cost equipment. I was most hurt by this unjust dismissal, but as with most things in this life, there is usually a silver lining, and so it was in this case.

I had been offered a job in a pub in Belsize Park near Hampstead, and decided it would be good for a change. The Roebuck became my home for the next nine months, and again, this experience was very rewarding and educational. I had time to explore the goodies on offer in and around London. I frequented the Festival Hall, and my favourite, the Albert Hall, and had so many memorable evenings at these and other venues, that I can only mention a few.

Meeting Yehudi Menuhin after a concert in the Festival Hall, was one of the most memorable, for he was one of the most humble men I have ever met. He was genuinely surprised that five or so youngsters had waited an hour to see him. He stayed and chatted for some time and, without considering himself, took a great interest in us and what we felt and thought. Interviews I have seen since confirm the impression I had at the time; his humanist views related to my later mentality. I also saw Toscanini conduct in his last years, from memory, and seated on a stool. The work eludes me now, but I am fairly sure it was Beethoven. I feel privileged to have had opportunities to see some of the real greats of the music world, and hope to see many more.

By this time, I had started a collection of records (vinyl), and would buy often on the look of the cover. One such purchase proved to be a lifelong passion, and is still in my possession. A ten-inch LP of two movements of Josef Suk's 'Asrael' symphony set me into an appreciation of that music that has never wavered. I have since had two versions of the full work, one on cassette, and one recently on CD, both by the Liverpool Philharmonic. It has been an inspiration and tonic for me over all the years since, the story behind the music being an integral part of its magic. Both sad and inspirational, it reaches parts other music has not reached. When feeling down, it lifts you up, and if you can hear it live, it will make you weep. Such was the case when I heard it live at the Albert Hall in later life, the sounds still ringing in my ears, the emotion still reverberating through my body. I was approached at the end of the work by a lady inquiring why I had had such obvious enjoyment from the work. I explained that it had been a long standing favourite of mine, and politely enquired her interest in this. It seemed her son was principal cellist in the Royal Liverpool, and she would pass on my thanks to him and the orchestra. I thank them again here for the indescribable pleasure that has been imparted to myself and, I am quite sure, a host of others.

A footnote to this part of the journal is that many years later, at a concert in Llandaff Cathedral, I heard Josef Suk, the grandson of the composer, playing a work by his grandfather, and he kindly signed the cover of the record I had. So, if you ever see this record of mine, remember it is NOT the composers signature.

Another visit to the Albert Hall around this period warrants a mention. The work was Tchaikovski's 'Violin Concerto', played by David Oistrakh. I had a good appreciation of the work, having tried to play parts of it on many occasions, usually along with the recording. Fortunately no one has ever heard, nor would want to hear, the awful results of these attempts. I was sitting high in the gods of the Albert Hall, where very few had joined me. My usual emotional pleasure listening to this magnificent work made me totally unaware of my surroundings, and at the moment the last note resounded around the hall, I burst into frantic applause, and called out very loudly, "BRAVO" at the same moment. My outburst preceded the other applause by, it seemed, at least ten seconds. The embarrassment must have shown, but the joy of the occasion dispelled all feelings of guilt.

I saw no conflict between this music and another form, namely jazz, the traditional type. My favourite night-spot, was Ken Collier's club near Leicester Square, where many an evening was spent in the pleasant company of other jazzers, clapping, dancing and foot-tapping. I remember the all-night sessions, starting at around midnight, and drifting home on the early Tube at around 6.00am.

I felt completely safe at these gigs. In all the times I spent there, I never saw any aggro. This fact seems to have manifested itself in to many differing situations and activities. As this theme is close to my thinking and attitude to life generally, I am always looking at one sport, or one activity that shows a tendency one way or another. It appears to me that aggression seems always to raise its head when there is frustration, either with oneself, or with a situation. In sport, there seems to be a general theme of what is, and what is not a recipe for more or less aggression. Explosive energy in an activity, seems to drain away aggression. Examples are American Football, an intense musical experience, or any activity that involves much concentration. These observations have made me pro-active in my attempts to make my life as non-aggressive as possible. That trait in my earlier years caused many heartaches, both for others and myself.

Selfishness is one of the most difficult traits to dispel, at least for me, as for many years I was not even aware of it. As I began to notice it more, I had the subconscious desire to disbelieve my discovery, thus making the solving of the problem infinitely more difficult.

Where and when all these forces in my mind started to take hold, I simply can not say. It has been a long journey. This means that placing these comments at this stage of the book may be premature.

My one regret on this subject is that I did not make progress along this track much earlier in my life. I am quite sure I could have avoided much pain and discomfort to others. Conversely, it may have changed many of my life's activities, and I may never have embarked on this, and many other avenues of discovery.

Enough of these distractions. I move on to yet another episode. Summer was fast approaching, and another opportunity had been set before me. Not returning to Leysdown-on sea, I had a chance to work in Torquay and Paignton in Devon, at a holiday camp, working for someone else in my chosen profession. It seemed like a bit of a holiday while making some money to perhaps fund another adventure; and so it turned out.

I began work at Barton Hall holiday camp, a beautiful location on a hill above the town. A series of chalets surrounded a magnificent old house, which had me thinking of Toad of Toad Hall again. I remember always being tired, a result of non-stop work, but I loved it. Again it seemed I was the only staff member capable of all the necessary tasks, and so, yet again, I was the main worker. I must point out here, that I would not have had it any other way. I sincerely believe it stood me in good stead in many of life's challenges.

In the second or third week at this location, I met a wonderful young lady whose name, embarrassingly, eludes me. I became hopelessly infatuated as only the young can. She was on holiday with her mum, and the situation was perfect for an affair. The affair was the most innocent of early encounters, and, looking back, was doomed from the outset. We met approximately three times at the camp, got engaged on the day before she left for home, and only on two occasions did we meet again. Beware of holiday romances: another lesson learnt.

My boss at the time had the contract for two camps, Barton Hall and one in Paignton just a couple of miles away. I would be whisked to and from the camps, helping keep the money rolling in, but eventually was transferred to Paignton permanently. My lasting memory of my boss, (his name escapes me), was his car; a VW Beetle, with its distinctive exhaust noise. Why do we remember such mundane facts and not the names of the people?

Towards the end of the season, I persuaded my parents to come on holiday to the camp, and a strong feeling of pride surges through my mind at the recollection. It was one of the rare times when I could talk on the same level, especially to mum, who was very clever and loving. My brothers and I never knew any of the everyday hardships she had to endure, she simply did whatever was needed, without ever complaining. Their holiday was a revelation for them and for me, and, on reflection, I wish I had done more to repay them for all their sacrifices for my brothers and me. I am sure these sentiments will strike true to most readers.

By now, I was becoming confident about travel. My friends who had said they would join me in a big adventure had decided to take different courses of action. So it was to be a onesome. My original intention was to make a circumnavigation of the world, but realistically I intended to take things as they came, and adjust to each situation.

Heading East

Most plans were in place for me to set off on the big trip. I had put together as much money as I could, around £80, a money belt for safe-keeping, passport and, of all things, a Webley air pistol as some form of protection for myself. My rucksack was grey and not very big, as I really intended to travel light. I had sewn a Union Jack onto the back of same, in a display of nationalism that I would now not consider appropriate. I had made some investigations into how to start my journey, but it only amounted to a suggestion by a friend that Asian hostels in London would often advertise for passengers to fill cars returning east.

Something that has haunted me from this period was that I had not involved my parents in my preparations, or considered their feelings in this matter. I had simply seen what I wanted to do, and had gone for it. On the morning of my departure, the urge to go was overwhelming. Adrenalin pumping, I left, almost forgetting to say goodbye, walking down Common Hill and onto Merthyr Road to head for Cardiff and then London. I still remember the spot where I was first picked up, no more than five minutes into my journey.

My thoughts now on this subject brings me close to tears as I think of what my parents must have gone through. Their fears and concerns at the dangers they knew were out there.

The next two or three days are a blur now, but I reached London and found two Asian hostels in quick succession, both of which had advertisements for return trips to India and Pakistan. The second one I tried offered a seat to Lahore, Pakistan, if I was prepared to help with petrol costs. I agreed, and arranged to meet my fellow passengers in Ostend in two days time. It seems they had bought the vehicle on the continent, and arranged to collect there, so saving some costs. When we met for the first time the car owner explained that his hope was to get the car back to Pakistan where it would have an increased value. I agreed a sum towards petrol and oil costs, and met my travel companions, two from Pakistan, and a businessman from India.

The car was a Vauxhall Cresta, large enough to accommodate the four of us in what seemed at the time to be reasonable comfort. I had never been an avid reader, but for some reason had a book to read on the journey, *1984* by George Orwell. I have to admit to looking over my shoulder on more than one occasion. Maybe *War and Peace* would have been a better option, or a biography of one of the great composers that had captured my imagination in previous years.

Belgium, then Germany, passed in a flash without incident. This is probably because they were familliar from my previous trips. When we reached Yugoslavia, things started to become new and exciting. I spent a little time at the border, confirming documents, but eventually we made our way past the checkpoint and into Yugoslavia. It was hot and our windows were open, we had slowly gone no more than a hundred yards, when I heard a voice call out to me, "Derek, where are you off this time?" I looked back only to see someone with a rucksack fading away. He shouted something about Abercynon to me, but that is my only memory of the incident. I should explain that Abercynon is a town just three miles from my home town, and even though I have spent most of my life in and around this area, I have never found out who that person was.

By this time, we had settled down to a routine of sleep, drive, sleep, with only one or two overnight stops at B&Bs. One day however, we noticed a car in some difficulty on the road ahead. It was travelling very slowly, so as we slowed down to pass we heard some cries for help. They were obviously ladies in distress, and I persuaded my friends to stop and see if we could help. It was now I discovered we had no tool kit for the car, not so much as a screwdriver. As I was the only one on board with some knowledge of the workings of motor vehicles, and having been greeted with such enthusiasm by the three Australian ladies, I decided this was an opportunity not to be missed.

My travel friends were more interested in food at this time, so they left me to it. I listened intently to the story the girls related on the problem with the car, and it became clear that it was a clutch problem. Having had some experience with my now deceased 'TIZA BUGA', I ventured under the car to try to discover the cause of the problem. They luckily had a tool kit and with a little huffing and puffing, I managed to adjust the offending clutch, giving them a little time to get to a garage and a probable more permanent cure. They were very appreciative and the cuddles I got on the roadside were very welcome, even more so when they asked if we would follow them to a campsite they were heading for.

Zagreb was the destination, and the campsite was close to a garage. With the agreement of my travel friends we made our way in convoy. Their car behaved on that short journey, and on arrival, we were all invited to join them for a meal. I don't recall whether my friends accepted the invitation, but the girls cooked up a great feast that evening, much appreciated by me, followed by conversation long into the night. One young lady in particular stands out (the driver if my memory serves me right), a jolly and cheerful girl who, in different circumstances, would have been a target for my advances. To her and her two companions I send greetings from the old country. If you recognise this story as your own, then do get in touch – but only if your car is now in good order.

The next adventure was just around the corner. We were approaching a small town, still in Yugoslavia, where we were halted by the police or military, it was difficult to tell. A lorry parked a little way ahead was smoking ominously. We sat and watched as the situation progressed. I got ready with my camera, a 35mm Balda, and took the odd shot. The fire service arrived. To our great amusement, it consisted of an ox drawing a cart full of sand. I decided to get a closer vantage point, and left the car to approach the incident, camera in hand. As I did so, the firemen were shovelling sand into the engine area of the lorry. One chap decided to open the door of the cab, hurling sand into same, when wham! an explosion and ball of flame billowed from the cab, hurling him to the floor. I don't know if he was badly hurt or not, as uniformed men rushed towards me, clearly angry at my use of the camera in this situation. I made a hasty retreat and luckily did not have my camera confiscated. However, we were very quickly ushered away from the area. On reflection, the Tito regime was in full swing at the time, and photos published would have been a little embarrassing to his country. He need not have worried. All my films were eventually lost before they were even developed.

In Greece, we stopped in Thessalonica. I took a walk to keep the circulation going. In those days, I did everything at full speed. If I could run I would, but on this particular day it was a mistake. I crossed a road and decided to hurdle the high kerb onto the pavement. Not a good idea. The pavement had just had white concrete poured, and had been left to set. Up to my knees in concrete was not what I needed on my first visit to Greece, but it did give some amusement to one and all. As much as I try to remember the immediate occurrences around this incident, I can not, this seems to apply to so many of the documented facts, which seem to stand out as snapshots of my past.

It was a frame of mind that dominates the next part of the journey, with no visual recollections, but a feeling of real excitement at heading for Turkey. I fully expected this to be an adventure into a completely unknown world. In reality, the only obvious difference to me was that there were more animals used in everyday life than I was accustomed to. It was the only aspect that troubled me at that moment, as whether used for drawing carts or as domestic pets, they seemed very badly treated. This was the first occasion I realised that we are all on this earth, struggling for the same thing, a good quality of life. The good people of Turkey, and, indeed, every country I visited, seek the same existence.

Istanbul was the real start of the adventure, with its magnificent Blue Mosque and Diamond Mosque, whose architecture rivalled anything I had seen in Europe. It was also here that we encountered a major stumbling block, in that no visa had been obtained to travel through Iran. With many visits to the Embassy, we were delayed for several days, giving us time to delight in this amazing city. Regrettably, my only recollection was the growing unease in my stomach: dysentery, the start of some very uncomfortable days. It began when we crossed the Bosphorus on a ferry. A cheese sandwich was certainly the culprit. It proved to be the start of a series of attacks right through to India.

There are no recollections of the difficulties there must have been during the next stage of my journey. It must be that we forget the bad and remember the good (not a bad idea). It was about then that we were given a warning by the Turkish equivalent of the AA that when we reached the mountains of Eastern Turkey, we should be very cautious and vigilant, as there were reports of shootings and hijacks. The favourite tactic, apparently, was for someone to lay on the road and make you stop, and they would then attack you. We were warned that they were armed, and not particularly shy of using their guns. I have to say that we did not encounter any such incidents. On the contrary, we were well treated wherever we went. The terrain of this region is very distinctive and the footage of Afghanistan and Iraq, so frequently seen on TV of late, reminds me so much of that particular part of my journey.

Ankara had been left behind, but I have to admit there are no recollections of that passing, perhaps my stomach condition blocked any memories that may have lingered from then. One incident that occurred after we left the capital, was the only time I reached for my gun. It was at a remote town somewhere, in Eastern Turkey or Kurdistan, with myself in the later stages of my second attack of dysentery, and the three friends gone off for some food, I was left in the back of the car to rest.

I was half asleep, when I became aware of people around the car. When I showed little reaction to their being there, they began reaching in to the car from both front windows, and I instinctively reached for the pistol in a poach in the front pocket of my anorak. No sooner had I taken out the gun, and to my undying shame, pointed it at a very large bearded gent leaning in the driver's window, the entire group dissipated, like some kind of magic. They ran in all different directions. I saw no-one until my friends returned. They were as bemused as I, and an explanation they suggested, was that the locals had wrongly assumed that I was secret police. The truth will never be known, but I think they were just curious at the arrival of a rarely seen modern car, and wanted to touch the dash and instrument panel. I can remember the face of the recipient of my aggression, and I apologise for any trauma I may have caused him and his mates.

Next was Iran, and I here have to admit to a lifelong admiration of the Iranian people. They were the most welcoming and friendly people I came across on my travels. That said, there are so many others that come a very close second.

My one and only book now took centre stage. *1984* needs no introduction, but it must be understood that in 1962 it was in the realms of science fiction, a sobering idea of what might be the future. It took my mind off the stomach pains that were continuing to trouble me, and remains one of the very few books that have lasted in my memory.

Before we reached Tehran, I saw one of those special vivid pictures that stay in my mind. It was dusk on a typical warm evening as we drove, slowly as usual, through the mildly hilly region, and exited a broad uninhabited valley, swinging slowly left around and down past a hill on our left. I remember staring at the sight that confronted me. Time seemed to stand still as I viewed the magical sight of dozens of little dwellings on the hillside, all with flickering lights in their windows. The almost dark surround so affected me, that the image is as strong today as it has always been. I need never return to see this again, as it is permanently fixed in the private photo album in my head.

I have had to stop writing for a short while, as the memory of this incident is quite overwhelming. Again, the act of putting these recollections on to paper is an experience I have only just begun to savour. I really wish I could share this image with everyone, unfortunately my camera stayed in its case, and the light, and the physical ability of the camera would not have been able to record such a scene. Such is the advance in technology, that today it would have been a doddle.

We arrived in Tehran and I found, to my amazement, a city typical of Europe. There were shops and stores selling the same stuff as we get at home, ice cream cornets readily available. It was not long before I sampled some. We spent a couple of days there, and at the time I did not recognise the shaking experience we witnessed each day as being mild earth quakes. No one there took any notice, so we followed suit.

Everywhere we stopped, I would be approached, and people, always men, (rather worrying), would want to try out their English on me. But more than this, they were genuinely interested in where I was from, and why I was there. I was invited many times to join families and share a meal with them, but strangely not my travel companions. One young chap was so interested to learn and practice his English he would follow me and chat at every opportunity. I suspect that my appearance was a little bizarre for their culture, as I had a bushy ginger beard, and wore an anorak with pockets everywhere, a little reminiscent of the military. I seem to remember we exchanged gifts when I left, and it was something very mundane that he wanted of mine, a coin or something, although I can not remember exactly. He, however, had made a pen knife from old springs from car parts, and seemed delighted that I was pleased to receive such a gift. The fact I remember it so well proves it was well received. I trust he went on to have a good and happy life. I am always bemused when I see news from this part of the world showing unrest and conflict, because I am quite sure that people like him are only interested in peace and happiness.

We stopped at a small village and found a place to sleep the night. I say this, because it is the only time on my travels that I remember staying at a set place. It was a round, red building, like a huge igloo, with a similar entrance, and a series of domes on top. It gave me the impression it was made out of clay. When inside, it was cool and spacious, with rolled up sleeping mats around the periphery like the points of a clock. It was amazingly cheap, a mere couple of pence (or equivalent) for the night, and surprisingly comfortable. The floor was soil but beautifully clean, giving us a very welcome night's sleep. Having slept mostly in the car to this point, I am sure most readers will appreciate the pleasure this offered.

To this point, we had one or two punctures, but always in a situation where a garage was available to repair. That was now to change.

Most of the roads we travelled in Iran were mere tracks, some of which were rutted very badly. It was no surprise when we had a puncture. I remember it was quite late one evening when we had changed the wheel, and headed off towards a small town some 50 to 60 miles on, where we could repair the puncture. Bang went another tyre, at least an hour from any habitation, back or forward.

By now it was almost dark, and there were no vehicles about to give assistance. Even more importantly, we were out of water. If that was not enough, we were having difficulty starting the engine. It seemed to me that the distributor was out of sync. We had no tool kit other than a screwdriver that I had acquired and the tyre changing tools.

The night was long and very dry. We were all desperately thirsty, and I was considering the water in the radiator for an emergency supply. The others did not concur with this at this juncture. On reflection, I think they were right, as with the lack of tools, and the possibility of doing more damage, we may well have ended in deeper water. But I read quite a few pages of *1984* that night, and thought the horrors of Room 101 in the book may be still preferable to dying of thirst.

At first light, the situation with the car was assessed. It was clear that we were entrenched in a very deep rut, and would have to move the car before we could effect a wheel change, and before that, would have to get the car running again.

More to the point, we could barely speak let alone work as our mouths were swelling up with lack of fluid. One of my travel companions suddenly exclaimed, "there is a workman way over to our right". It was a worker doing some kind of repair work, on what, we will never know. One of my mates decided he should go and ask for some water, as he spoke a little of their language. After some time he returned with a clay cup of water for each of us. I do not think I can explain how we felt when we drank, very slowly, every little drop of that sweet nectar. The colour of that water, muddy brown, would normally put anyone off drinking, but in those circumstances it was the nectar of the gods.

Equally importantly, our provider of water agreed to take the punctured spare to the next village for repair. One of our group accompanied him.

Now to solve the next problem. The engine would not start, so priority was the distributor. I tried thinking about its simple mechanics, remembering the things I had learnt when tinkering with the old car, and the BSA motorcycle. But when I started to dismantle the distributor, I quickly realised that I really did not fully understand its intricacies. However, I cleaned and checked what I thought were the main workings, and scraped the contacts of the points. I reassembled and reconnected as best I could, crossed my fingers and would have prayed if I had been so inclined. Any amateur mechanic who has ventured on similar endeavours will know the feelings of mostly hope that purvey the soul at such moments.

I felt like a genius when the motor purred into life. Shortly afterwards, our companion returned with the repaired tyre, and more water. Soon we were on our way. I sat in the back of the vehicle with my Indian friend, feeling quite smug at my part in our rescue. My third cat-life was gone.

We arrived at a small village late one evening with a tyre needing repair. We found a workshop with a mechanic still in attendance, although it was well after dark. He readily agreed to see to our needs. We left him to complete the task in his own time. At home, arriving at most garages after closing time would result in a negative response, but here we were welcomed with a smile and a genuine desire to help.

I realise, of course, that they probably did not get all that much business in such a small village, and the chance to make some extra money would be welcome. But I have to say that they were very eager to help, and most jovial, chatting with my friends, who could converse to some extent in Farsi. They were also very keen to try to converse with me. Unfortunately, my linguistic abilities were very limited, and we reverted to mostly sign-language to communicate.

We were right on the outskirts of the village, and by now it was very dark. Try to imagine earth roads, no street lighting and an unknown void beyond the last buildings. It was at the very edge of the street where the mechanic worked on the car, and some of the young locals had gathered to meet and talk to these strange travellers. One of them had a donkey that he rode with some prowess, and was very eager to give any horsemen (or should I say donkeymen) a chance to show off their skills. I'm no horseman, but still volunteered to have a go, not suspecting for a moment there could be any repercussions to such a trial.

Wrong, yet again. No sooner I had made myself comfortable an the animal's back, and taken hold of the chain reins attached to the donkey, when I heard a loud cry and massive slap on my steed's rump. Off went the animal into the night at some speed, the laughter of the audience rapidly fading out of ear-shot. I hung on manfully, hoping the animal would get fed up with this tedious game, but no chance. I think he could see freedom at last, with or without me on board.

It was pitch black in front of me, and the thought raced through my mind that a massive drop may be dead ahead. As I could see nothing at all, I considered the options; fall off, or keep trying to stop the charge of the heavy brigade. To my great relief, the fine specimen had run out of hay, and decided to come to a dignified halt. The crowd had tried to follow, and were quickly on the scene to applaud my fine efforts, and return joyfully to the village. Much merriment was displayed by our hosts, and it continued for some time after the event. On reflection, I am sure the whole sequence probably only lasted a few minutes, but it had seemed endless to me. As you, the readers can tell, it has lasted long in my memory.

Another incident from this part of the trip was when we travelled through what seemed endless, faceless scenery. We saw a dark cloud some distance ahead, lingering over an oasis of green and brown. This soon became the next small town of just a few dwellings, and the dark cloud was a mass of flies. It certainly focused my mind on not eating at this oasis when we became aware of the food market outside each shop on the main (only) street. The other notable observation was that the only sign that I could recognise was Coca-Cola splashed on several advertising boards. That, and other bottled drinks had long been a staple source of liquid refreshment, as I thought, and was probably right, that they were less likely to aggravate my delicate stomach. Incidentally, the reason for the recurrence of my bad stomach was a lapse in my choice of food some days earlier, when I really fancied an omelette at a roadside café, big mistake.

The last adventure in that wonderful country of Iran was the last 500 miles or so, as we left a hilly section, in searing dry heat. We swung around a hill, and were about to descend into a massive bowl of a desert, at the far side of which was a conical mountain that reminded me of a picture I had seen of Mount Fuji. Capped in snow, it seemed surreal in the temperatures we were experiencing, and yet there it was. It seemed in easy reaching distance. Not so, as we travelled all that day and more before we reached and passed the landmark.

This turned out to be the last lap of the long trek to Pakistan, with another lasting memory of this desert region strong in my mind: dozens and dozens of miniature whirlwinds twisting away around us as we drove towards the border. It was as though the occasional white puffy clouds were playing with yo-yos creating a massive playground for this little used area.

Perhaps here I should try to explain the interaction between me and my fellow travellers. The car owner and his friend were going back to Pakistan after working in the Britain. They were returning to wives and families in Lahore after a year or so in the UK. Apart from this knowledge, I had little interaction with them. One thing that sticks in my mind is the curious habit the driver had. As he drove, he would be constantly clicking his tongue on his teeth, making a very strange noise, almost non-stop. It reminded me of a similar noise made by my father, which would drive me almost to distraction. His was caused by poorly fitting false teeth, and the tea table occurrences would often lead me to a swift disappearances from the table.

There is little else remaining of these two in my memory, except that one of them had a link with a photographer in his home town, some miles north of Lahore. He had agreed to get the photographs I had already taken processed to negative stage, so as not to allow any deterioration to film subjected to excessive heat. When we arrived in Lahore. I was asked to stay with the family of the second gent from Pakistan, before moving on to India. The driver went off in his car to his home north of Lahore, with my films, which he said would be returned before I went on my way.

News was received some days later that he had returned to his home to find a very bad situation had occurred while he had been away. His wife apparently had left him and his reaction was, unfortunately, the most severe that can be. He killed himself. Life is full of great tragedy as well as joy, and this story still sends great sympathy back to his memory, even though our paths only crossed for a brief time. My films too at that point were lost forever. C'est la vie.

Back to the third gent, who accompanied us on this journey. He was a businessman from Bombay, returning after some dealings in London that had obviously not gone to plan, thus the difficult return choice of transport. He was a tall, and very well spoken man, with a wonderful mastery of English, a man who took great pride in possessions. The gold rings and the suit gave that away, and his interest in one of my possessions was to turn out to be of great value to me.

Despite the incident I described a few pages back, I cannot understand now why I'd thought packing a Webley .22 air pistol was a good idea. When resting during the journey, I would occasionally try a little target practice. My third companion was very keen to take part, always saying he would buy it off me if I should ever want to sell. So it was, that when he left us in Lahore to journey on to Bombay, he gave me the equivalent of £12 for the gun and my tin of pellets, which turned out to be enough to pay my train fares for most of the rest of the journey.

India & Back

After my short and most enjoyable stay with the family in Lahore, I set off with a freshly washed set of clothes to witness more wonders of this amazing world. I said farewell to my Indian companion, and decided to head for Amritsar and its famous Golden Temple.

This encounter turned out to have, and still has, a profound influence on the way I have changed. At the time I was simply ashamed and angry when I learned of the infamous massacre of hundreds of men, women and children, when British troops opened fire on an unarmed gathering. The fact that it seems to have been an accidental order given by one person, does not distract from the horror that ensued. I am sure that the story has been well documented elsewhere, and I am certainly not qualified to make any comments on the incident, but if we can learn from such mistakes, perhaps there will be a better future for all.

The well into which many jumped to escape the bullets was still there at the time, and many bullet marks in the outer walls of the temples, clearly highlighted for posterity. I remember walking for a long time, in disbelief of an incident that I had had no knowledge of. It still saddens me today. While there, I spoke to many of the locals, who did not seem to have any lasting animosity towards their old masters. On the contrary, they were very complimentary of the legacies that had been imparted by the British occupation. At the time I had not thought this too important, but as I grew in my experiences, I started the process of acceptance; that when violence is followed by further violence, it promotes the old chain reaction. This was further reinforced when I began to learn of the actions of Mahatma Gandhi. The shrine here is adjacent to the stunning sight of the Golden Temple. These Sikh Temples, going back hundreds of years, which I had the privilege to see in their original state, were utterly superb.

The large square lake was surrounded by numerous Temples decked in gold. I found it incredible that there could be such massive wealth openly on display, guarded by Sikh guards wielding an ancient pike-like weapon very similar to the Beefeaters at the Tower of London. I felt privileged to be able to walk amongst these priceless treasures, albeit with a handkerchief to cover my head.

In the middle of the lake there was a bandstand, reached by a long walkway. At all times there was music being played, which I found most pleasing and peaceful. I am told that the music is constant all day, although I only have an unknown observer to thank for that information, which may or may not be true. Some years ago, the Temples were destroyed in a religious motivated action, and have now been reconstructed close to the original.

Next stop Delhi, the amazing Parliament building in its red brick, and the long walkways up to its entrance, will live long in my memory. It was close to here that I visited a kind of club where dance lessons were being given by a British couple to very beautiful Indian girls, but no boys. On my appearance, I was quickly approached to take part, but my footwork was not of a good standard, and my scruffy appearance was not conducive to my participation, although I have to admit to being very taken with the sheer beauty of the ladies.

I was certainly not in this stunning place to find a wife, but to savour the meeting with a nation of which I had no knowledge, only a preconceived picture of what I would find. That picture was one of a superior, surveying a nation of poor and underdeveloped people. To my shame, I continued in this superior attitude for some time. What I did not know then, was that my experiences there would teach me more than any other experience since.

I got accommodation in a youth hostel close to the centre and close to a Buddhist enclave. This was the first contact with a group of people that completely unwittingly changed my life. At that moment it merely struck me as so peaceful and that they were unhurried in everything they did, smiling a lot of the time. It took more than two decades to realise that there was something in their way of life that could pertain to myself, and it was around this period that I heard a saying 'Know yourself and you will know others.'

I have repeated this so many times to myself and to others. It is so simple in this frantic world of 'Fast'. There is a simple truth in some things. It does not rely on ancient texts which have supposedly been written by great teachers of the past, but rather states the obvious, if only each individual cares to look at themselves.

Enough of philosophy for now. I must here try to paint a picture of sights I saw in and around this great City. First a local ancient set of temples that I thought were called the 'Qutab Minar'. It was an overgrown area, full of ancient buildings and temples in a very sorry state of repair. I walked through this site many times during my stay, witnessing young children and families playing and walking. Some children took part in an activity that was more than a little dangerous. One of the tallest buildings was two or three storeys high, of stone construction rather in the shape of the Eiffel Tower. There were steps up to the different levels, and at the base and in the middle was a deep pool. The children would climb the steps and drop down the centre into the pool. It seemed a very dangerous activity to me, but gave obvious enjoyment to the participants. This is another of those places that has left a clear image of the area, including the winding pathways through the ruins, and even the type of stone the monuments were made of. It was this clear image that made me try to retrace my footsteps some years later when I attended a wedding.

That will come later, but let me continue the story of my Delhi visit. On one of my walks into the town centre, passing along the pathway through the old Temples, and walking along a long highway flanked by tall trees giving some welcome shade along the way, I experienced a sad and disturbing scene. A funeral was making its way slowly along the highway, when the horse pulling the hearse reared up, depositing the coffin into the road. As it did so, the coffin burst open, revealing the corpse. The trauma to the family must have been considerable, and yet the calm way the situation was sorted had to be admired. Before long, all had been rectified, and the cortège continued on its way.

Little more remains in my memory of the city of Delhi. Probably because very soon I got a third attack of dysentery. This time it meant business and I was laid up for some days. I had a sleeping bag over wooden boards in the hostel room where I had stayed and with no others staying there, it really was not the best few days.

One advantage of few people about, was that I did not have to queue for the toilet. I use that word somewhat loosely, as we would not recognise it as such here in the UK. The excessive discomfort of these few days cannot adequately be described, but I do remember being very positive in my attitude, and was confident it would pass, as did everything I ate and drank during that period.

What made these few days so interesting and educational was the view through the glassless window. Opposite the hostel was the Buddhist enclave, where monks went about their daily tasks, and seemed to me to be in complete control of themselves, with a happy disposition, and a constant smile. I do not pretend that it had an immediate effect on my outlook on life, but it had sown the seed of change in me that would take decades to manifest itself in my every-day life. If I had recognised the value of what had been put before me earlier, I firmly believe I would have made fewer mistakes in my travels through life so far.

Slowly, but surely my energy returned, and I was urged by someone at the hostel to attend a doctor's surgery to speed up my recovery. I took their advice, and when I eventually got an appoint-ment, the doctor informed me that for 25 rupees he could cure me. I only had about 15, so I had to let nature take its course. Fortunately, it was not long before I felt able to take the next step on my journey.

Bombay was calling me, but that was a long train journey away. My hopes to see the Taj Mahal en route would have to be curtailed because of cost and my still weak body. Anyone who has travelled on the wonderful trains of India, will know the excitement and frustra-tions of such adventures. I had the choice of first second or third class travel, and the cost would be crucial. Not only cost, but the difference in comfort was a significant consideration also, as I had been well advised by someone on my travels that the scramble for third class seats was more than a lottery. It was just within my pocket to travel second class, and it proved to be a very good investment. So I took to the road to the station, leaving the recollections of my little haven by the Buddhist enclave to enhance in my memory for decades to come.

On reaching the station, it seemed the whole nation was on the move. Bustling crowds filled the concourse with sounds that I find it difficult to describe, but the excitement of the chatter reminded me of the funfair at Barry Island on a bank holiday. The only cry to stand out, was that of the tea seller: "chai" "chai", the youngster with the metal cups and the large tea pot advertising his drink would entice any traveller to try his tea. I did for the first time taste the pleasures of the tea culture, and it was not the last, as it became a must at many of the stops along the way. Part of the reason for my change in choice of beverage, was on the advice of someone else I had met along the journey, who pointed out the simple fact that the water had been boiled and was therefore much safer to drink. I must have been very slow not to have worked this out for myself much earlier. Better late than never. It was the beginning of the end of my dysentery.

I have a memory of the arrival of the train, which was a proper train, with smoke and dirt and noise, and a very leisurely pace, which gave many of the locals a chance to run towards the incoming loco, and climb in through the windows, doors or any other means of getting a good seat in the third class compartments. I subsequently learnt that window glass had long gone, as it would only get broken in the scramble for entry to obtain a seat. It all seemed very dangerous to my eyes, but to my great relief, the second class compartments were almost empty, and it seemed no one had been hurt. It remains a mystery to me how people travelled in such discomfort without complaint. I am sure another lesson was being planted in my subconscious.

Most of the trip was, and still is, a blur to me, as the only recollection of the actual journey was a brief view of the Taj Mahal in the distance (or did I dream it?). It was to be some 44 years before I would visit this magnificent building, but that first brief view still remains a vivid and moving picture in my mind.

Still very weak, I arrived in that iconic city of Bombay. It was to be a stay full of incident and learning that has affected much of what has happened in my life since. My original concept of what I expected the people and places to be, I found totally wrong.

I searched for somewhere to stay, and looked up the Indian fellow traveller who had gone straight home to Bombay after our arrival in Lahore (once he got his hands on my Webley .22). Then I acquired a room in a youth hostel, which apparently was the accommodation for the students in term time for the University.

What luxury this was. There were showers, and a bed that was just a little more comfortable than the one in Delhi. I quickly took a shower, much needed after the long, hot and tiring journey. There were, to my knowledge, no other residents at that point, and my room was some 20 yards from the row of three or four showers. I covered my embarrassment with the one and only towel I possessed, flung the towel over a beam between the showers, and soaked for some refreshing minutes under the cold, and welcome downpour. I was standing on white tiles with a wooden surround, and I thought the best plan was to dry off here and not risk meeting someone on the way back to my room. I remember the silence was quite deafening, but as I dried off could hear a rustling noise. I ignored it for a while, but got curious and looked for the source. It became obvious after a while that it was emanating from under the wooden base of the door. I really thought it must be the plumbing or the water escaping. I peered under to find a sight to make a mere westerner cringe. It was a large group of cockroaches fighting for the right to eat me. My feet leapt at least a foot in the air, the door was flung open, and I disappeared down the corridor to my room waving my towel behind my naked frame.

It had been the shock of the discovery more than the actual sight, although I have to admit I have never seen such large cockroaches before or since, and the noise they made as they fought each other was a surprise. Showers from that time on were undertaken swiftly and in sandals.

In all the time I spent in this, and other accommodations, I remember meeting no individuals specifically, but I must have done so, as many years later I was contacted by someone who remembered me from that hostel. But that is for a later disclosure.

The sights and sounds of Bombay, have, I am sure, been far more eloquently described by others; but I will attempt to give my interpretation of this amazing place, in the way I saw it. The calm vibrancy of the street activities, with animals, bikes, scooters, cars, carts and most of all people, wearing a mixture of traditional and western dress, captivated me. I was drawn towards a society that I simply had not expected. I was still somewhat aloof as a 20 year old, swimming in this new ocean of sights and sounds, searching for the knowledge to transport me through this life that was opening up in front of me.

The smells can only be experienced, but the sounds that confronted you from every quarter were revolutionary to me. The glissing of the singers, with their high-pitched voices, seemed to hypnotise you with a melodic consistency that drew you into a sense of well-being. It seemed that every shop or household, on every street would be playing their own choice of music. The overlapping of these, created a constant drenching of sound, the subliminal effect of which, resulted in a permanent liking for the overall efffect.

Strolling the streets of Bombay, as it was in Delhi, was a pleasure day or night; the daytime gave one a clear picture of the relaxed, yet frantic pace of life. This now seems a contradiction to me, and yet it reflects my take on what I saw and felt. I passed one particular scene, on more than one occasion, where the women were washing the clothes. It was a vast sunken area, with rows and rows of separated, stone washing areas. There were women and children beavering away, each in their own little space, washing and rinsing the clothes. All could be surveyed from the high vantage points around. The area would have covered a football pitch, but made me think of paddy fields, with the water carefully channelled along to each individual wash area.

Another daytime vision, an everyday event, was the interaction with the beggars. I use the word, beggars, as it is the only easy way to describe them to you, the reader. I would, however, describe them as some unfortunates, who, for one reason or another, had dropped into this way of existence, sometimes through injury sometimes by choice. The most distressing to me were the children. They acted as individuals, but if they saw another have success in getting a rupee from a tourist, would flock around, usually very gently I have to say, and would begin the constant cry of, sahib, sahib, (sir, sir) hoping for further offerings.

Coming to a routine in such circumstances did not take too long out of necessity, but I always found it distressing. Even more so were the regular attentions of the disabled beggars; some of their disfigurements were quite horrendous, with twisted or missing limbs a regular feature. I remember learning from someone in the Salvation Army there, that some would deliberately disfigure themselves in order to be able to beg. I can not confirm or disprove these allegations, but if it were true, it paints a very disturbing picture.

Let me here describe specific characters I can remember. The first I saw on more than one occasion. He had a completely withered arm, with no sign of life left in it. Another had no legs and a very short body. He was perched on a board with wheels on each corner; his hands were mere stumps, wrapped in cloth, that would propel him at some speed along the streets, sometimes in and out of the traffic. He could only have been two feet from head to floor. How he survived is a mystery to me. One feature I remember very well was the gentle tug on your sleeve or coat, accompanied by the plaintive, sahib, sahib. I must stress here, that in this, and subsequent visits to this wonderful part of the world, I never felt threatened in any way by these, or any other of the peoples of this great continent.

I feel obliged here to relate a final description on this subject. It occurred on another visit, but that is superfluous, as it seems there is little change in these matters over the years. I was travelling in the back of a car through heavy traffic, in the middle of one of the big cities. We were surrounded by the usual mixture of bikes and cars travelling slowly in all directions, yet a strange poise was displayed by all, locked in this very common situation. We had been stationary for some time, and I had been watching the face of a young Indian lady on crutches. She had one leg only, and the stump of the lost leg was being supported by another crutch. There was very little room between the vehicles, but she would somehow work her way between them, very slowly, but with great poise. None of these attributes were the reason for my fixation on her. Her face was the saddest sight I have ever witnessed. Her eyes mesmerised me, and as she made her way towards our car, our eyes met. Her outstretched hand, and dark, sad eyes will haunt me for the rest of my life. I wanted to embrace her and comfort her, but I knew that was not possible. After what had seemed a lifetime, but which passed in a moment, she was gone, melting into the boiling pot of life; not, however, without the ten rupees I had managed to pass to her.

I cried then, and have done so on many occasions since, when reflecting on this moment of life. Her eyes were those of a dead woman, and yet she went on, never knowing the impact she had on my inner self. The compassion this one encounter has generated is something I would never have thought possible, and it would be very interesting to know if the story could be comprehended by others. I have to admit to being quite drained by the writing of this episode, the emotion of which requires some time to reflect and redirect the mind; and so, I shall continue after the indulgence of a coffee break.

At night, the city drifted into an eerie silence. As it was so much cooler, it was the time to take a walk to savour the strangely uniform architecture of the city. Many of the residents chose to sleep outside because of the heat indoors, and I walked around and past many families snoozing on the pavements. They all seemed to stay very close together, and it was very clear as to why when I surveyed their surrounds. Rats were in abundance all around, criss-crossing the streets wherever I went. They seemed to me to be of a giant variety, unless this is my memory playing tricks. All this seemed quite normal, and I treated it the same way, as I followed their example and frequently slept outside.

I had by now moved to a hostel with the Salvation Army, where I met Major Bennet and his family. I recall none of the geography of the hostel, or, indeed of the family, but I do have the highest regard for their unselfish devotion to their fellow man, regardless of their religious persuasion. They have remained the only group in any religion that have retained my admiration to the present day. It was here that I was told of a group of volunteers that had set up a retraining centre for the poorer people, mainly the beggars of the city. Its location I do not remember, but the impact remains. It seemed to be based on a medieval village, in that there were huts around the periphery of the site, all making different items to be sold. The workmanship was remarkable, and considering the number of disabled people involved in some very difficult skills, the end products were amazing. They made cushions, leather goods of all types, pottery and many more objects of art that escape my memory, but all had given the 'Beggars of Bombay' a chance to escape the inevitable end that came to most of these unfortunates.

I purchased what I could, and on return to the UK, passed on all but one object to friends and family. That one object is still in my possession, namely, a leather cushion, cleverly decorated with strips of different coloured leather in an extraordinary pattern. I am sure that the scheme improved the lot of only a small percentage of those in need, but the results to those who were the recipients must have been life changing. I would hope that the scheme is still changing lives for the better. My admiration goes out to those who were, and are involved in the venture.

All these encounters during the days in India, were imperceptibly changing the way I thought, none more than the regular sighting and study of the 'Fakirs' or holy men who seemed to be everywhere. These Hindu gurus were extraordinary individuals who seemed to defy the laws of life and physics by remaining in one position, the Lotus position normally, for great lengths of time. One in particular was stationed very close to the hostel. Each time I passed him, I would always acknowledge him but the most I got back was eye contact sometimes and an occasional very slight nod of the head. Aren't our memories amazing that such apparent superfluities are stored in our brains. This particular gent was clothed in traditional Indian dress and had his face adorned with patterns of coloured designs. It is in my consciousness that the lessons I was learning then took a long time foor me to turn to my advantage by beginning to recognise 'Self' with a greater degree of confidence and acceptance.

I was beginning to think of home, or maybe the possibility of trying one more adventure before returning to the UK. Australia was comparatively close, and if the opportunity arose, I just might contemplate that option. Money was now a major consideration, or rather the lack of it. I had been offered one job as a photographer while in Delhi, but refused as it would have curtailed my itchy feet and wanderlust somewhat. I considered looking for a job there in Bombay, but soon realised my mind was turning homeward. I started looking for ways of getting home, or at least moving on. I inquired with the British Embassy who said I would have to be completely destitute to be aided to return home, and would then have to make restitution of the cost on return to the UK. It all seemed a bad idea to me, and a bit of a cop-out, so I became determined to find a way on my own.

Here started a new adventure in determined, and uncompromising actions to find a way home, without the use of money. Down to the docks to search for a ship returning to Europe. Easy, or was it, no way baby; it would take patience, luck and a great deal of persuasion to achieve this plan. First off, I checked the boats in the docks.

I attended a maritime office and inquired of times of departures and destinations. Here I met one or two Indian gents who were sympathetic to my dilemma, and tried their best to help. We discovered two ships that would be leaving in a few days, and had a destination that would get me in close proximity to the UK. They also suggested I try a British ship leaving in one or two days. Assuming the British boat would be my best bet, (this says much about my prejudices at that point), I got permission to enter the docks, provided I left my belongings at the docks office. I did so, and made my way to the berth of the first choice. I managed to see the captain, but was very quickly told that there was no chance on his boat as the crew were all Chinese nationals, and he was not permitted to take on anyone. He made it clear he was not interested in taking chances, and implied that it would also be very dangerous for me.

I took the hint and departed, somewhat bemused that a fellow Brit was so offhand about my request. Next on my list was a Norwegian freighter, and their captain, a Mr. Anderson, struck me immediately as a very private man. He spoke very quietly and with a superb knowledge of the English language, but he was also a man of few words. He pointed out that he could only take me on, without pay, if he received the OK from his head office in Oslo.

This noted, I went next to the Russian boat, where I received a more boisterous welcome. It was immediately obvious to me that Vodka was the most important passenger on this vessel, but the captain's welcome was warm and genuine. He again explained the difficulties of getting permission to take me on, but did not exclude the possibility. Progress, but still a long way to go. I returned to the dock office where I struck up a friendship with one of the staff. It was to prove invaluable in the scheme of things, but for now I had to try to get permission from one of the offices of the ship owners. My friend had explained that there was increased security at the docks, due to the conflict going on on the northern border with China. This said, he felt it was the best bet to try the Norwegian head office first in Oslo.

I was by now very short of funds, but spent a few rupees on a telegram to Oslo. I had a few days before the boat sailed. I was confident I would get a positive reply to my request, and I was determined to use the few days to see more of this fascinating city. The next day I went a wandering close to the Gateway To India, a large and prominent arch on the coast, visible from way out to sea, and a very well known landmark. Having packed my few belongings for my departure, and put them ready at the Salvation Army hostel, I was travelling light, and had wandered much further on this day, determined to see as much as possible before departing these shores. The wax merchants were in profusion, all along the sea front, busily removing wax from the ears of eager clients. If you have not been to this great continent, this may be a mystery to you, but let me assure you, these surgeons of the ear lobes are very skilled. I did not avail myself of their skills for a few reasons. One, I had no money; two, I had no knowledge of how skilled they were; three, I could see absolutely no benefit of such a procedure. I bought another hand of bananas to feed my now reasonably settled stomach, that being the cheapest nourishment available. Intermixed with the ear doctors, were, of course, the snake charmers, often attracting groups of tourists and locals to witness the mesmerising of the magnificent cobras. To stay and watch a performance would cost a couple of new pence (naya passa), this being the equivalent of one hundredth of a rupee. I watched at a distance and kept walking. Their little wicker baskets reminded me of the laundry baskets from back home, the lids being firmly replaced when the snake had finished its performance.

A variation on this theme was also occasionally to be seen, the setting of a mongoose against the cobra. This street performance was not to my liking, as it depended on the owner of the mongoose pulling the mongoose away at the last minute, as it lunged for the cobra. It was, of course, using the natural instincts of the only animal quick enough to beat the cobra. Somehow I felt great sympathy for the snake, which, although a deadly reptile, has just as much right to exist as us.

My feelings expressed by this statement were soon put to the ultimate test. It was mid-morning on the long walk day, and I had travelled inland from the Gateway to India, and come across an enormous field, dotted with groups of cricketers, young and old, exercising their passion for that sport. There must have been several games going on at the same time, and I simply wandered around the long grass of the outfield. I would occasionally stop to watch a particular bit of action, not yet realising that this game would one day play a considerable part in my life.

It nearly did not, for as I watched, I heard a hissing noise. I looked around me, and then down to find a coiled cobra, hood flayed, poised to strike. I cannot tell you what went through my mind in those next moments, but it seemed a long few seconds as I worked out a strategy for survival. Should I bolt for it? I thought not. Should I try to reason with it? I thought not. Perhaps I should make a hurried Last Will and Testament, or maybe have a very close look at this most beautiful creature, before departing this world. No, as the cold beads of sweat burst through my forehead, I decided stealth would be the best strategy; and so it was. My first glance at the cobra was my last, for I stared straight ahead, very slowly lifted my left foot and moved slowly forward, before raising the right foot nearest to the snake even more slowly, and taking "one short step for me". The cobra never flinched, obviously realising the danger of being infected by biting such a scruffy individual, and so he or she lived to bite another day. One more cat-life gone, that makes four.

The next two mornings I attended the dock offices for news of my request to Oslo, but each time there was no news. It was now getting critical. I had abandoned the other ships, and thrown all my eggs in this one basket, so after a chat to my friends in the office, I decided to spend my last rupees on a final telegram to Oslo. The ship was due to sail the following day at mid-day, and trusting in my sheer determination to go with this Norwegian ship, I brought my pre-packed haversack to the entrance to the docks, and waited for the reply to my telegram. My friends there were most helpful and looked after my kit while I went to the office of the Norwegian shipping company to see if they had any news. They had not, and with a heavy heart I returned to the docks office, at the entrance to the docks, to see if they may have received any news direct.

The image that stands firm in my mind, is that of one of my friends from the office, waving furiously at me with a sheet of paper in his hand, his left hand I seem to remember. "Got it", he cried, and my heart leapt. I will never know if that piece of paper had anything written on it or not; I only know that this guy in the office had made a huge contribution to my journey home.

"Off you go", he said, "you only have a few minutes before the ship sails." Thanking him and grabbing my haversack, I sped the half mile or so to the ship, the captain on the bridge, preparing to sail. All my belongings were at my feet as I indicated that the paper had arrived with a thumbs-up, and to my great relief he beckoned me on board. So often have I thought of those who helped me at that critical time, but in the great scheme of things, it gives me a good feeling about my fellow man, and has reinforced my faith in humanity on many a dark moment.

On board, and feeling very content with myself, I stood on deck as the crew did all the necessary casting off, and we slowly made our way out to the open sea. It seemed that I stood still, as India moved away from me, and I think I knew at that moment that I would return. The Gateway to India so slowly dropped over the horizon, and I was still there on deck, the light fading away to prepare for the next day.

From then on I was provided with food in great quantities. I am sure they thought I had been starved almost to death. I was given accommodation in a small cabin, which was to be my home for the next weeks. I was given tasks on board, generally painting or scraping, and got to know the crew who were Spanish and most cordial to me. One of them more or less adopted me. He would relate his family details, and how he missed them while at sea. He also saw to it that I was kept safe from the heavy drinking members of the crew, and would get me extra work from the crew members needing clothes washing. This was the only way I could get a little money together, to get me home when we eventually docked in Europe.

The smell of diesel was a familiar smell as we sailed across the Indian Ocean. When not painting or scraping I could savour the delights of the open sea, often watching the antics of the dolphins criss-crossing the bows of the ship, with that typical smile on their faces. In the Red Sea they were very prominent. It was the start of a lifelong admiration of these fine, intelligent animals, culminating in a swim with two of them while on holiday much later in Malta.

In the first days on board, I was treated to a galaxy of culinary delights, making up for the months of under-nourishment along the diverse routes of my travels. It soon became obvious that the large intake of nourishment was not being complemented by the necessary removal of the end product, and it was some days before I thought it necessary to get some medication. I was given a liquid to encourage movement, but without success. On my second visit to the first officer, he gave a wry smile, and produced the smallest tablet I have ever seen. "This will do the trick". He was right! It took fifteen hours, but the results were nothing if not dramatic. I had been lulled into a false sense of security, as there had been no signs of movement, and so I went on deck watch, at the pointy end. This was in full view of the bridge, and as suddenly as a sneeze would arrive, so did the need to get to a toilet. No chance, it was too late, with my rear end trying to direct the outslaught through a gap for dispersing sea water in a gale, the amusement on the bridge must have been immense. So was the relief to my system, and after a few more sessions at a more usual venue, I returned to normal.

Suez Canal was the next encounter. And what an encounter: I could never have imagined the enormity of this amazing feat of engineering without seeing it first hand, but I will not attempt to describe anything but my view of the scene. The lasting memory is of us apparently standing still, and the pyramids floating by. If you ignored the water in the foreground, the effect was stunning. The water was like a millpond in the lakes at the centre of the canal system.

I remember being very sad about the attacks that had been made by us Brits to try to keep control of the canal. It seems a shame that such damage was done to the actual structure, and to all the parties in the conflict. I clearly remember the feeling of loss, towards the people who died or suffered, and now realise that it had changed my feelings to an empathy for all who suffer in such times, not just the one side.

Port Suez was to be a stop for our vessel, and we were instructed that no shore leave would be allowed. It did not affect the crew as it was to be a very short stop, and as I was not on duty at this juncture, I took advantage of an opportunity to do a little bartering with the local traders. The little row boats would come alongside and call up to anyone who would listen, offering to swap trinkets and souvenirs for watches, soap, and it seemed, almost any item available in the West. They all spoke some English, and I started a trade through the porthole of my cabin. I explained that I had a watch that needed repair, but would trade for a model camel. The deal was struck and the complicated system of first throwing a rope up to me, and then a basket attached to the rope would be available to pass items to and from their boat. All seemed normal until the moment my watch was on its way down to them. Suddenly, the items coming my way were quickly pulled back to their end, but my watch disappeared into their clutches. I tried in vain to hold on to the rope and effect a recovery, but it was a fruitless attempt, and my last view of the two men on their boat, was a frantic, yet smiling retreat to the shore. Another experience locked in the old brain.

Our next port of call was somewhere in Spain. I regret that I remember only being there, and going ashore with one of my fellow shipmates for a quick look around. No other recollection remains, although it was around this time that the captain spoke to me for only the second time, saying that his ship would dock at a port in Holland, and would then travel to Gdansk in Poland, then return to Antwerp. He continued that I was free to leave the ship in Holland, or travel on, and I opted to see a little of Poland, and travel through the Kiel Canal, with a tentative plan to leave the ship at Antwerp.

And so on we went through the English Channel, up the North Sea to the Kiel Canal. When we entered the canal, it was a still evening with a severe fog, and the entire journey was spent to the accompaniment of the deep tones of the fog-horn. My job was to remain at the pointy end to signal any visual obstacles to our progress. It turned out to be quite a hairy trip, the constant call of one fog-horn answering another. In the end, I saw very little of the canal, but again the experience was rewarding.

Arriving in Gdansk, with the weather about to deliver a Christmas storm, was uneventful to start, but when deepening clouds slowly hovered over the city, and the snow storm got under way, it looked like a wonderful white Christmas was about to unfold. The snow started in the early morning, slowly increasing in intensity. By mid-morning it was a sight to behold. Vertical lines of solid snow flakes were building a snowfall of unrivalled beauty, such as I have not seen since. Within the space of fifteen hours, the snow was at least three feet thick, but long before the end of the storm, the captain had instructed a group of us to keep the bridge clear. We shovelled and swept for hours, clearing an area each in around half an hour, and then starting again. I have never experienced such beautiful snow, yet had no chance to enjoy the more sporting aspects available at such times.

The next day I was alone on deck still clearing snow. It was then I first noticed the guards along the quay. It seemed they were Russian soldiers complete with rifles, part of the Russian occupation forces. I really fancied a snowball fight, but did not think of the consequences to my actions, mainly due to my youth and arrogance. I launched a very well directed solid snow-ball at the guard, and achieved a bulls-eye, striking him on the back of his helmet. I have no idea of the unsuspecting guys reaction, as I cowardly took cover below until things settled down.

We spent Christmas on board, but did make the odd excursion into the town, where myself and one or two of the crew would brave the snow, and go for the odd drink. I noticed the beauty of the ladies that I saw, with their distinctive cheek-bone structure. The only thing I remember about the men was their dislike of the Russians. When I mentioned the name of Khruschev, there was a noticeable silence. This town was the birthplace of the Solidarity movement, with Lech Walesa many years later.

We set off back through the Baltic. In the quiet moments I remembering my father's journeys across this same stretch of waters, so many years earlier, sending out his Morse code messages from a ship that must have had a similar look to the one I was on now. Next stop, Copenhagen, and we arrived to find the docking area iced over. It was very thin. We went like a knife through hot butter, but it is the only time I have seen the sea frozen. I was soon ashore to view the city, and the first thing to see was the famous 'Mermaid on the rock'. It overlooked the quay where we had docked; quite a shock to find it was a mere two feet tall. The bronze figure also seemed to be damaged, the head looking as though it had been twisted. It turned out that it had had its head re-made, after it had been removed by thieves. All in all, it was a bit of a disappointment, but on reflection, good things sometimes come in small packages.

We stayed only a day or two, but did manage a ferry trip to Malmo in Sweden. It snowed the whole time we were there, but it seemed to be the norm by now. Nothing more to report here, but it was now that I had to start thinking about leaving the ship, and heading for home. I had a couple of good mates on board, and they were planning to repay me for all the washing and ironing I had done for them during my working voyage. I had no knowledge of it at that point, but was busy planning my last few miles back home. I must here point out, that names of my associates on this long trip, must be conspicuous by their absence. The facts are, that I simply cannot remember them, a trait that has dogged me all my life.

Had my original book survived, I would have had some of these documented. I had kept a red, hard cover book for many years, a record of my journey written as I travelled. I stored it in case my children, or any other party would be interested in reading this hand-written record. Unfortunately when I moved to my present abode, it got lost. Luckily, this brain of mine retained enough to make a fist of this journal. How fortunate have I been, to have existed through the comparative calm of the fifties, sixties, seventies, eighties, nineties and now into the next century.

Early morning, Antwerp, grey snowy clouds hung over our vessel. I had been reliably informed, that as I was not an official member of the crew, I was never on board, and so could not be discharged. I had therefore to simply 'jump ship'. The captain looked the other way, but the crew had made a little surprise for me. Because they cruised the oceans, stopping at so many different ports, and changing money to so many different currencies, they accrued a stock of coins that could not easily be changed. I received a huge bag of coins from the crew, with the vital information that I could change these for sterling at Thomas Cook in London. My one friend also gave me one of his old pairs of woollen gloves that would prove invaluable despite the holey nature of the same.

I walked down the long gang-plank to the quay, waved a tearful farewell to the few Spanish crew that I had got to know, and, I am fairly sure, noticed the very private captain, peering from the bridge.

He had done me a great service, and I will always look back with affection at his kindness and humanity. To the crew, I am sure I do not have to spell out my gratitude, as they did not have to accept me in the way they did, or give me such support. The memories they left with me will warm my thoughts in old age for many a year.

As I started my hitch-hike to home, I reflected on my success in returning to Europe under my own steam, and remembered all the fine people that had contributed to my safe return. In particular, the Indian friends in the office at the docks in Bombay, and the captain of the freighter. But, for now, it was how to get to Calais or Ostend to return to the UK. It was before noon, on the 31st. of December 1962. Snow was still in the air, as my thumb prepared for some serious hitching, and it was some miles before I got my first lift. I was set down some time before midnight. That heralded the longest hike without a lift of my career. Heavily laden down with coins of many realms, I enjoyed the hooters and sirens noisily seeing in the New Year, somewhere out on some country road, in some country close to the English Channel. I walked until after noon, on January 1st, my ginger bushy beard in serious need of a trim, until, eventually a lady driver took pity on my forlorn figure, and gave me a lift in a warm welcoming vehicle, giving me renewed energy for the final push to the finish. After another footslog of some hours, a gentleman, who spoke very good English, was going some way towards Ostend, but in the end took me all the way to the ferry, even though it was well out of his way.

Another thank you from one of my many prayer flags fluttering their messages into the atmosphere. I barely had the fare to return to Dover, finding a few coins in my collection to reach the required amount. The white cliffs were buried under a considerable fall of snow, and it was a little surreal as we docked to see so much white. It was as though I was entering a clean, new, white beginning.

Feeling quite smug and satisfyingly superior at my endeavours, I began the trek towards London, looking forward to the release of the great weight of the coins, for some funds to get a hearty meal. The snow had made travel very tricky for the motor vehicles, and the lack of traffic was going to make the journey to London more difficult as a result. Walking up a slight incline, that swung to the left, I noticed a lady sweeping the snow from the path of her house. As is my usual way, I struck up a conversation with the lady, and ended up helping her. Soon her neighbour saw help at hand for her driveway, and before I knew it I was given a shovel to clear a few of the paths. This was after the daughter of the first lady had emerged from the house to offer me a pair of gloves, as she could see the state of my holey, woollen gift from the sailor.

I accepted the gloves with thanks, and spent the next hour or so bending my back. Job completed, and with remuneration for my labours from grateful neighbours, I returned to the first house to regain my pack, and chat briefly to the mother and daughter. They had already gleaned some of my travel story earlier, and said they had prepared some food for my journey to London. It was nicely wrapped, and as I left, I looked back to see the daughter in the window, our eyes met for the last time, and I regret to this day not writing down the address, or the phone number. Sometimes it is better this way, yet all these years later it still brings a tear to my eye, more so when I remember what I found when I opened the food package. There on top of the cake and sandwiches, was my fully darned pair of gloves that she had swapped for the work gloves. So many wonderful people in this world, and yet the bad always seems to be the only news we ever see and hear with the media.

The hours that followed were spent pushing cars, sliding along white roads towards my goal. It was quite late when I eventually set foot again in the capital. Where I stayed that night I cannot remember, but I received a reasonable amount for the stash of coins donated by the friends aboard their floating home, by now far out to sea.

The urge now was to see my family and friends again. Having eaten and cleaned up a little, I started the last hours of this great adventure with a sense of pride and excitement at the prospect of all that was to follow. I had hitched to Cardiff, so decided to take the luxury of the steam train the twelve miles to my hometown of Pontypridd. The green green grass of home, and the now white hills, gave me the safe feeling that only a homecoming can give. I was broke, but happy, and as I walked the last mile to my home at 4, Mackintosh Road, The Common, a strange calm was apparent as I walked through the open door with words of "Hi mum, I'm home".

Home to Work

It was as though I had not been away. Mum cooked a meal, and life was back on track with much story telling over the next weeks, but no great emotion shown by anyone. I had arrived home with a three-penny bit to my name, and that coin is still in my possession.

If this story makes anyone a tenth as happy as it does me, I will feel that I have translated a little of the great feelings that flood my memory, and fuel my desire to even more adventures in the future.

Over the next months, I was asked by a number of organizations to give talks on my experiences overseas. To my surprise I managed this with some degree of success. Although so much time has elapsed between then and now, I still feel able to relate the stories, sometimes with an extra touch that was not present in my young introvert mind.

I was now earnestly seeking a more settled stage in my life, and thought more and more about a stable job, and a partner to spend the rest of my life with. At least that was the thinking, but without the knowledge of relationships long term, I was entering a new concept in sharing; something I had not encountered to this point.

Before I got into this mode, and before setting up in business, I continued travelling to the Continent occasionally, but in short bursts, choosing random destinations usually at short notice. Most were of little interest, without any need to document them, but one that does stand out was in reply to a newspaper advertisement, where grape pickers were needed to harvest the crops in France.

It was a student thing really, but I thought it would be interesting, and arranged to join a group in a town called Santenay near Dijon, 'Couper le raisin' (harvesting the grape) was our sole duty, although a little wine tasting might also be necessary.

This trip was to be mainly by train, and with my old friendly haversack from the India campaign, plus a newly acquired one-man tent, I set off first to Dover, then Calais, and on the wonderful French rail network to Dijon. I arrived here too late to get to the village of Santenay, and decided to camp the night somewhere near. I walked a while, and eventually left the town, and went up a fairly steep narrow road in complete darkness. When my eyes got used to the conditions, I could just make out a gate and a field beyond. Great place to pitch the tent I thought, and with the help of a very dim torch, I managed to get sorted, climbed into my sleeping bag, and was soon in the land of nod.

Just before dawn, I was aware of a rustling noise outside, and sleepily peered out to see the source of the noise. "Sugar", or some similar word whispered through my lips; it was a very large bull eyeing me up a short distance away. I vacated the tent in somewhat of a hurry, and leapt over the gate I had entered from the night before. The bull maintained a presence close to the tent, as though he was telling me something, and I was in no mood to argue with him.

Fortunately for me, the tent was green and not red. Unfortunately for me, the farmer whose field this was, arrived wielding a shotgun, and informed me that I should leave his field "tout de suite", or invoke his wrath. I did not understand all that he said, but I certainly got the message. I quickly removed my tent and belongings from the field, under the close scrutiny of the bull, who had shown admirable restraint, much to my delight.

I returned to the town and continued the journey to Santenay by bus. The town was small, and the farmhouse where we would stay was in the middle of that town. There was a church, a square and a stream flowing close to the road. The image in my mind is still strong of the farm itself, and particularly the back of the building, with the stone steps to the bunk-house on the first floor where we slept.

We all ate together at an enormous table. I have a lasting image of the first meal we had there. Plates were distributed to everyone, then a large plate of potatoes placed in the middle, and everyone took a share. There was then a pregnant pause as most awaited the other vegetables or meat. Our hosts started eating so we all followed, and when that was done another large plate of vegetables arrived, and was duly shared out, with the same continued eating. Finally, the meat arrived and that was shared and devoured by all. This has been the only experience of such an eating custom, but I have to say it was a very pleasant one.

Work in the vineyard commenced the next day at a very early hour, and the ten or so Brits trooped off on the back of an old truck to savour the delights of harvesting the beautiful grape. It took no time to discover why so many workers were needed to do this work. The fields seemed to roll on for miles, in great horizontal lines disappearing into the horizon. With the help of the local workers we were shown the ropes, or rather, the vines, and we began the back breaking task of reaching over the three foot high vines, to find the ripe bunches of fruit. We each had a basket, that systematically would be collected and deposited in great vats on the trailers behind the tractors.

We started at the end of the field, with each picker having a line to work on. The ignominy of our poor picking ability was quickly in evidence, as the locals would be a hundred yards ahead of us in no time, some of them very elderly, and some no more than children. They were, however, more amused at our incompetence, than troubled or annoyed. They would regularly come and help us catch up, and were most jovial in demeanour.

I was, at this time, primarily a water drinker, and we had been reliably informed, that the water in the area was strictly for washing. This could easily set me on the path to alcoholism. The wine that was provided in vast quantities quenched my thirst and the desire to work. Combining the need to drink fluids, and 'couper le raisin', became a juggling act frequently in conflict with each other.

Apart from the agonising pains in the back, that struck all us Brits within a day or two, we all took to the cultural bonding with gusto, and joined in the celebrations that seemed to take place every evening. I think we did less than a quarter of the work the locals did, but it was never an issue, and we were accepted as we were.

One day, about a week into the project, we had made an early start as usual. As it was a particularly hot day, it was important to keep the fluid levels up. Oh boy, did I. I can remember the usual pain in the back abating somewhat, and a happy disposition taking over my being. The grapes seemed to find their way into my basket with consummate ease, but it was soon evident that most simply fell into the aisles between the vines. I battled on as best I could for a while, but eventually succumbed to the alcohol, and collapsed over the vines into the next lane. I have no idea how long I was in this predicament for, as the rest of that day is a bit of a blur.

The work was punctuated with a day off, when a few of us went to a local bathing spot for a swim. The river was their swimming pool, although not very deep, it was the most welcome distraction, and good therapy for the back.

I took no photographs at this, or many of my other ventures, and it is another blank in the memory box. Towards the end of the two weeks at the vineyard we helped in the preparation of the wine, tipping the vast quantities of grapes into the vats, and turning the massive wheels to lower the press. The one thing I remember of this process, was the taste of the thick juice, the first product that could be tasted. It was more like syrup, very sweet and sticky. What I cannot remember, is whether or not this liquid was potent.

The one thing everyone wants to have a go at, is the treading of the grapes after the main press has done its job. This we did have a chance to witness, but were not permitted to join in. The locals would link arms and trudge around the vat, getting the last drops of juice from the grapes. It is, I am sure, very reassuring to all you wine drinkers, that the bare-footed workers, would always wash their feet; after doing their trudging.

The journey home was the usual laid-back affair, not really wanting to get back to the drudgery of making a living. I had been offered a job in a processing lab in Cardiff, with a Mr Hurley in Pearl Street, Splott. He did black & white processing for many of the local chemists in and around Cardiff. I was needed as someone who could take on almost any of the tasks involved in the trade. The volume of work he got through daily made me realise that there was a market out there for someone starting out, although I could not see how I would be able to afford the start up costs at the time.

I settled in to the routine of early starts, commuting to and from Ponty on my motorcycle. I began the habit of working odd hours here, as it was typical of our trade to have to get jobs done, when and where they occurred. One evening the boss asked if I could have a go at fixing a blue pane of glass that had broken. I worked on to concentrate on this one issue, but did not take any reasonable precautions against possible damage from the glass. In particular, I did not wear protective glasses, and sure enough, a piece of glass flew into my eye as I was chipping away at the surround. My eyes water when I recall this incident, as I knew immediately that I should not blink and cause more damage. It was an uncomfortable half hour travelling to hospital for treatment, and a huge relief when the doctor said, "Success". He commented that it made the job easier because the glass was blue. I trust readers will never be as stupid as I was on that occasion.

Working overtime one Saturday morning, I was left alone to get some films processed, while the boss closed the shop to run some errand. I was the only one in that morning, and went into the basement to set up the deep darkroom for the batch of films. What follows still haunts me.

I must first explain the function and layout of the room. It was a darkroom within a room, taking up half the space. It was entered via a light trap, which is a door, a two-foot gap, and then a curtain, forming a light trap for entering without light affecting the processing. There was a foot high ledge along the length of the narrow room, to stand on in front of the five feet deep tanks for the developer, rinse, fixer and final wash. First I had to unwrap the films and clip them onto rails of three, with up to six rails. These eighteen films would then be lowered into the developer in sequence, all this process in complete darkness. A touch clock would then be set for the appropriate time for development. During this part of the process, we had to stand by this tank, still in total darkness, and systematically agitate each rod of films for about ten seconds each for the six or seven minutes of this first part of the process.

The silence at this stage was total, and on this occasion, the silence was interrupted by someone brushing my back, and whispering something in my right ear. I paused for about two seconds, and then called out thinking one of the boys was playing a prank on me. Another two seconds and I threw myself back off the ledge, arms outstretched until I hit the wall, hoping to find the intruder; there was no one. I could not turn a light on as it would ruin eighteen films, so I hurriedly covered the tank of half processed films, and exited through the light-trap to find the perpetrator. There was no one. I re-entered the darkroom, and hurriedly moved the films into the fixer, and switched on the safelight. The room was empty. I called out, and ran throughout the building, but all three floors were silent and uninhabited.

When Mr. Hurley returned, I related the story to him. His reaction was just a little vague, and I never felt comfortable in that room again, getting one of the others to carry out those tasks wherever possible.

This apart, I learned a great deal working there. It stood me in good stead when I eventually acquired a similar business of my own. For now, along with a friend, I undertook a little fun project. Derick Ebbsworth and I had been friends for some time, generally chasing girls at dance-halls, but suddenly decided to take on a motor project, after acquiring an ancient Model T Ford. The engine was old, and only 850cc so we decided to up the ante, and fit a 1200cc engine.

I cannot remember how long this took us, but I recall many long hours in a quarry garage in Cilfynydd, grinding in the valves, fitting piston rings and many other skills that have long deserted me, and, I suspect, Derick as well. We eventually got the motor running, and the power for that time was considerable, and spent many a silly evening showing some of the posh cars how to speed away from lights, and overtaking, where I am sure I would not do so now. These were carefree days and unknown to us then, were very formative, the skills learnt there serving us well over the years.

That car eventually died through over zealous driving, when the block cracked, and the engine and car were sent to the knackers yard. I am sure this was mainly my fault, and I trust Derick has forgiven me after all these years. He did give me the honour some years later, of being his best man.

Speaking recently to Derick, he reminded me of an incident that occurred, when he and I took my old green Ford van on a trip to the Gower. We slept in the van on air-beds. Unfortunately for Derick, his had a puncture, resulting in a very uncomfortable night for him. It may also have been on this trip, that another incident occurred. We were going through the main street of Pontypridd in the van, and we had also painted white walls on the wheels, oval on the front, and square on the back. This optically made for much amusement to the onlooker, and on this occasion we were passing the New Inn Hotel, and stopped at a zebra crossing. A somewhat inebriated gent came out of the bar, watched our vehicle pass slowly by, and silently, turned and re-entered the bar. What had gone through his mind is all speculation, but the image of the event sits firmly in the mind of Derick, if not mine.

Those few years before marriage were the last of those carefree moments, that only reopen when, and if, one is lucky enough to have some late free years. I seem to be having such a time, and this is part of the search for some form of clarification of my "self", that has changed so markedly over the last ten years.

I think at this stage in my life, I was just beginning to appreciate that this big world is really very small, and most of the peoples of the world are interested in a peaceful, and purposeful existence, trying not to disturb other's space. It did take a very long probationary period for me to start the process of appreciating that my mindset was only mine, and that others had their own.

I have always thought that education in this country was inadequate, because it did not teach people to live, only to store historic, numeric, linguistic and artistic information, without teaching what I now believe to be of prime importance to us all, and that is to look inward at ourselves, and achieve peace. I cannot understand how I functioned thinking only of what I wanted, and not what I was.

It is only on reflection that I see how my perception has changed, as the middle years of my life were a blur of my fight to find an existence. I went through the motions without realising that life was running me, and not vice-versa. Enough of this searching, let's move on to the next adventures.

Settling Down in Ponty

During this period of frivolous youth, I had stored enough knowledge to consider starting a more permanent occupation, and between short excursions to the Continent and generally doing very little, an opportunity presented itself with a friend from Ynysybwl. Len Hudson had been running a business for some years, taking films from local chemists, processing, and returning them the next day. This was a local operation, identical to the business I had been associated with in Cardiff a couple of years earlier.

It seemed a natural for the skills I already had, and I spoke very nicely to the bank manager, and got a loan of £1,000 to buy out the business. I inherited the premises at Robert Street, Ynysybwl on a rental agreement, and the limited machinery therein to continue the operation smoothly. So continued my lifelong (so far) link to the making of a living through photography. Len had been in poor health for some years, but he remained there to advise and help where he could, and he and his wife remained friends.

My territory was from Church Village to Rhydefelin, Senghenydd and Cilfynydd, and the daily deliveries soon became routine. The building in Ynysybwl however, was rapidly becoming inadequate, and I started looking for a more suitable premises. Financial restraints did not seem to worry me at the time, but in years to come, the overdraft proved to be a burden which badly affected my life. This first major venture was to set the tone for much of my work ethic. The times I worked would depend on the demand, and in the summer, the demand was so great that night shifts were normal. Throughout my career, this has been a necessity, quite enjoyed by myself, but has caused difficulties for others. This fact did not register with me at all, and with hindsight, I could have avoided many pitfalls in my relationships.

I had a special friend – in fact, the person who first told me that

Kennedy had been shot – who has remained special to me, but could so easily have become much more than that. The hours I worked certainly clouded my judgement, and although I have no regrets at all, I am sure that if I had had a clearer view of myself, I may well have made different choices at the time.

This also applies to a previous reference in this journal, but really, it is only of academic importance, as what is, is. I am trying to say, over and over, that the blinkered, narrow view of the young only represents what they see, and that often is not the view of others. Old age has some unsavoury aspects, but the one thing it brings is an ability to see ourselves more clearly.

As I lived in Mackintosh Road still, I had decided to move the business to my area. This became possible with the discovery of a premises in Morgan Street for rent at a reasonable rate. It was a garage area between two properties, with substantial room at the rear. The back room was spacious and ideal for building a tank room at the end, similar to the one used in Mr. Hurley's place in Cardiff. The one hope was that the ghost from there would not follow me to this place. Luckily, no such recurrence was to follow, and the conversion of this new workplace was very successful.

It is fitting that I mention here the lasting ties I had formed with the considerable number of the Italian community in our area, most of all, Marenghi's Café on the old bridge in Pontypridd, where I became good friends with Bruno and Maria, and subsequently Maria's husband Bruno Mark Two. He would become Big Bruno, and Maria's brother Little Bruno. Along with this family, there were the Franchis, the Rabaiottis, the Contis, Bertorellis, and of course, the Cruccis. Many of these have remained part of my every day survival, with the Marenghi/Bertorelli Café in Taff Street giving coffee and food sustenance to me and my family for many a year. More recently, the Crucci Café, 'Park View' keeping the nutrition of my old body in good order, with almost daily doses of their fine cuisine.

I must pay tribute to Maria, that fearless young lass of the Marenghi family, who I witnessed take on a particularly obnoxious, and somewhat inebriated gent in their café one evening. The café had two entrances, one mainly to the shop area, and the other to the tabled café area. The young man in question was making a nuisance of himself in the café part, shouting at someone, with his back to the door. Maria took up arms in the shop part, went out through the shop door, and came in the café door behind the noisy gent. Wielding a pie warmer, she gave the guy one almighty wallop with the said instrument, that stopped the guy in his tracks, and got a warm round of approval from us in the café. The man was so amazed at the action, that he made a hasty retreat, and to my knowledge did not repeat his bad behaviour. As for the pie-warmer, it bore the scar of battle until it was replaced.

The premises at Morgan Street served me well for a number of years. It was around this period that my oldest brother Bill decided to move to South Africa. The firm he had worked for since qualifying from the Treforest School of Mines as an Electrical Engineer, was South Wales Switchgear. They had an operation in South Africa in Port Elizabeth, and he was very keen to start a new life there. He remained there for the rest of his life, marrying and having a fine family. We had little contact with him from this period on. Part of this was the fact that he was a very private sort of guy, and tended to keep himself to himself.

My other brother Bryan was a different character altogether, and was a salesman of some ability. He worked as a car salesman for a while, and moved on to pet food sales before some years later, also moving to South Africa to sell insurance, vertical blinds, and later to manufacture and sell pool tables.

Before he left, we had a short experience as owners of a Jaguar XK120 sports car. What an animal that was. We shared the running costs and the pleasures it had to offer, both were excessive, but worth every penny. When it was my turn to use the monster, I would behave like an aristocratic lord showing off his wealth. I have to admit that the pulling power for the girls was awesome. Perhaps I should resort to such excesses now to improve my chances (dream on).

At this point I had met, and begun seeing, an extremely beautiful young lady from the Rhondda. I remember the dance night all too clearly, when I watched the said lady coping very well with a drunken admirer and his advances. As he gave up, I moved in, and the rest is history. Although it was not the pulling power of the Jaguar then, we did, a little later, have an experience in the said car. Don't jump to conclusions, as anyone who has driven this model will understand. We were visiting my mum at Mackintosh Road, and approached the hill junction at Merthyr Road, to cross over and take the last few yards home. As I waited at the junction, I noticed smoke escaping from the bonnet. Within seconds flames also appeared. Elaine was in the passenger seat, and I suggested most forcibly that she should vacate the car and run well clear.

As she did so, and with the engine now dead, my only option, was to reverse the car out of harm's way, into Llanover Road. By this time the flames were considerable, and were billowing at front and sides of the bonnet. It was about now that the realisation came to me, that I was sitting above ten gallons of petrol. I do remember that adrenalin tends to make you act very quickly, or rather, it did me in that circumstance. I made the car secure and vacated the cockpit rapidly, rushing towards the main road for assistance. Luckily, a motorist had seen the drama unfold and was with us almost immediately with a fire extinguisher. The rest is a bit of a blur, but suffice to say the car survived with the electric choke identified as the culprit. No real damage had been done.

Some weeks later, I was on my way to my workshop in Morgan Street. At that time the junction of Taff Street and Bridge Street was all two way, and I was travelling across the bridge. I stopped at the junction and looked both ways before moving off, there was a blur to my left, and then a bang and a shout. My reactions were good, and I stopped immediately, I discovered a very small boy, and an even smaller bicycle on the road, luckily unhurt. Later, we worked out that the boy on the bike was lower than the bonnet of the car, and would not have been seen.

With help from some pedestrians, we got the bike into the boot, the boy into the passenger seat, and returned both to his home. On arrival there the mother came to the door, hands on hips, and uttered "not again". She was more worried about me than her son, who apparently was excessively accident-prone. I often wonder if he managed to reach adulthood.

In today's world of litigation, I can imagine I would have been done for several things including kidnapping, and yet I had done what most would have done, and correctly. The only addendum to this story, was that I heard that the boy had boasted to his mates, that he had had a ride in a Jaguar for his troubles.

I ran a Green Austin A40 for most of my runabout jobs, and one morning I left 4, Mackintosh Road to go to work. I was close to a lane to reverse into to exit the road, but with limited vision in the van, I did not take enough care in checking other traffic. Right hand down, foot down, and watch driver side so as not to hit the wall. Bang, the passenger side had hit something. It was the back end of the milkman's horse-drawn milk delivery service. The horse seemed totally oblivious to the incident, and there seemed no damage to his cart. It seems like a scene from a Dickens novel. My embarrassment was considerable, as a few people had seen the incident, and no doubt had well founded opinions of my driving.

The only grandmother I had known lived with us for several years. Her poise and restrained demeanour were a source of wonderment to me. Nothing seemed to faze her. Her calm was, I am sure, a result of her upbringing. Her husband had been a bank manager, when they were not glorified salesmen, and she had been a well-known pianist in her early years in Manchester. One story she told me on more than one occasion, was the time she, as a pianist, had been invited to a concert at a major venue in Manchester. It turned out to be the first performance in the UK of Edward Grieg's famous Piano Concerto. She told me she was sitting very close to the pianist who was none other than the composer.

She told me another fact that seemed remarkable to my twentieth -century mind, that she remembered very well the announcement of the death of Tchaikovski in 1893, when she was sixteen. It all seemed surreal to me, and perhaps it explains my strong links with music, and the pleasure I have always enjoyed through one kind of music or another.

I tried on more than one occasion to get her to play something on the old piano we had in the house, but she always refused, saying she had not touched the ivories since she was 50, and would not do so again; she never did. She did however live on to the ripe old age of 99. My mum and her sister insist she would have made the century, had she not thought she was 100 on her 99th birthday, fully expecting her telegram from the Queen on that day. She passed away peacefully in her sleep that very night.

Bryan, my middle brother, was doing quite well in his work and his golf. He had been club champion at the Pontypridd golf club five years in succession, and he and every other member of my family had success in the golf stakes at their club. All except me, and of this I have no regrets, but my association with them and the club still holds fond feelings, just so long as I do not have to chase a little white ball around a mountainside, an occupation that ruins a decent walk in my opinion.

A lasting image of Bryan, is the bowler-hatted salesman, with his briefcase in hand, driving off to sell some more of his cat and dog food around the many corner shops of that era, dotted around every village in the Valleys. As I mentioned previously, his retort to any shop-keeper who did not believe his boast of the quality of his product, would be to open a tin of Kit-e-Cat and eat it cold. I am led to believe it increased his sales considerably, but spoilt many of his amorous approaches.

His golfing years were cut short, when he was hit on the elbow by a golf ball. I was present at the particular moment, viewing from the tee of the number six hole at Pontypridd golf club. The driver sliced the tee shot that bounced just short of the seventh tee where Bryan was waiting to play. He was facing away from the incoming missile, and it bounced up and struck him on the point of the elbow. It seemed after a short while that he was OK but as time went by, he realised it had done more damage than he had thought, and his serious golfing days were over.

Here may I illustrate the naivety of our generation. It can be read into a story we would often repeat when boys got together. I am quite sure many of us, myself included, would not realise the full significance of the saying, but we would still laugh. It related to girls' stockings, and in particular, the band at the top, which I understand was to give the suspenders something substantial to grip to. The name given to this band was 'The Chuckle Band', as it was understood that if you got past that, you were laughing.

Needless to say, many of us did not achieve such pleasures. A kiss and a cuddle was generally the best you could hope for on a date. Of course, I speak only for myself in this matter, as I was of the old school. (You may believe or otherwise at this juncture.)

Visits to the local Girls grammar school were often a feature of my activity. One such visit nearly got me into hot water. I was to meet Jennifer and when I arrived at a pre-determined time, she would sneak away, and we would go for a walk in the woods behind the school. This practice was specifically forbidden, and if discovered, would end in detention for the girl, and a report being sent back to the head of my school. Luckily I had just left, so it was only Jen that would be in trouble. I remember hiding behind a red brick wall, after being seen by a member of staff, but we still managed a meeting a little later.

A year or so later, I was friendly with great group of girls mainly from one class. Although I did not venture too often near the school again, we would meet at local dances and socialise. One of the girls married my best friend, Derick. Both Derick and Margaret have been good friends ever since. Some of the girls in her class could quite easily have become more than just girlfriends. I do not think it would be appropriate to name these, but one at least will know who I mean.

I was living in a society still trying to forge a new path through the revolutionary progress of the post-war period, with new music liberating the minds and bodies of youth. Another artist of my generation lived in Treforest, and even at this early stage of his career, was widely regarded as one who must make it in the world of popular music. It took a little while, but as everyone now knows, he did. Tom Jones was a regular around the club and town scene, and our paths often crossed with my profession. Would that I had kept any of the photographs I took of him at the time. Sorry to say, I have none. It was only on one of his return visits to the town that I managed a picture of him on the famous Old Bridge. Regrettably, the paparazzi followed us onto the bridge, and produced a pint of local ale for him to hold, and the photo I wanted went out of the window.

I trust the following story will not offend Tom, but there was an occasion in Marenghi's café, when Tom left without paying for a cup of tea. Something I am sure we have all done by mistake; and on one of his visits to the town, I gave him a message from the owner of the café, Bruno, that all was forgiven, and he was welcome to use the café again. To his credit, he remembered my name, and acknowledged the remark. I cannot say I knew him well, as his music was not my preference. However the talent was universally acknowledged locally, and to his credit, he saw it through to total success. If you happen to read this Tom, there will always be a cuppa on the go, so call in, but without the paparazzi.

Another story that springs to mind was a visit to the YMCA of a certain Frankie Vaughan some years before Tom 'made it'. Frankie Vaughan cut the record 'Green Door', and had given the proceeds to the Boys Clubs Organisation. I vividly remember one of my pals Joey in many a photograph and sequence of film that I took of the visit, along with my mum who was quite a fan of his.

It was some months before, that I had met Elaine, and the wedding plans were well on track. I had become a regular visitor to Porth in the Rhondda, and it all seemed to roll along smoothly. It was October 8th, a Thursday, that we tied the knot, and the sunny, but windy day remains firmly in my memory, my brother Bryan as best man, with all the family and friends in attendance. It also says something, that I took some of my own wedding photos, even though there were at least three professionals present. We went to the Lake District for our honeymoon, a destination we were to visit many times in the years to come.

Politics had sneaked into my ambitions, but it was mainly a social thing at first. The Young Liberals were quite strong in the area, and soon I was pushed into the role of chairman, which only meant, an organizer. There was a small but vibrant group, with Ashley, Jean, Ruth, and Mr. Green, I do believe that most were there for the social side, but whatever, we made a lot of noise, and had a good time doing it. Most of the names elude me now, but I do remember the Raft we built to enter the Student Raft Race to Cardiff. It was the Taff-Tiki, and was run by the students in our area, starting in Upper Boat, some three miles south of Pontypridd.

It became an annual event, with considerable crowds attending, and taking part in the event. The crowds would pelt the rafts as they started with flower bombs from the bridges. Sadly it was soon to become a victim of Health and Safety, when one student died of an infection picked up from the water during the race. I do accept that the river was not as clean as it is now, but the fun of the event, and the challenges it presented in building the rafts, and manoeuvring down the fast flowing river, were a sad loss.

When we had built our entry for one of these races, we decided to test run our creation and do a little advertising at the same time. So, with a sail inviting new members to join us, we launched the vessel from the top end of Zion Street, and sailed majestically and very slowly under the famous Old Bridge in Pontypridd, where a large crowd had gathered to watch us pass. Various members took turns on board, sailing past Ynysangharad Park, under the foot bridge at Marks & Spencer's, where an even bigger crowd had gathered, then on, into the wilds of the Broadway towards Treforest.

I had my turn after the second bridge, and with several wet colleagues following our progress, we approached the small weir, half way down to Treforest. Don and myself were about to test the strength of the raft. No problem, and it was so successful that one of the girls wanted to do a re-run with her on board. So we managed to carry the raft back up river, and she got her wish, with my gallant self helping to keep her safe, as we got soaked at the bottom of the weir. We were all wearing life-jackets, and I am pleased to say that no one was hurt in the venture, and we got a few more recruits to our ranks.

I still occasionally watch the cine film taken of the event with great nostalgia, and I am sure it had a part to play in character building for all of us.

The big race, The Taff-Tiki, was a few weeks later, and we were full of confidence after proving the strength of our raft over the weir. We had successfully negotiated the shallows by jumping off and pushing, so we thought we were prepared for anything the river could throw at us. You do not need two guesses to know we were wrong. At least twenty rafts entered, some designed to reach only the nearest pub, and others with serious success potential. Our Raft was somewhat basic, made from six drums welded together, three on each side. They were lashed together, with wooden cross members, and one seat on each corner. The sail was quickly discarded after the first 100 yards as it was in the way. Our oars were simple, shaped planks of wood, that were obviously inadequate for the job. We pushed most of the first 200 yards through the shallows, or should I say the two of us boys pushed, while the girls had an easy ride.

Nearly all the other crafts were long gone out of sight as we struggled to get moving, but soon things settled, and we somewhat sedately sailed alongside the Treforest Trading Estate. I was sat astride the front of our craft, and we were making reasonable progress, when there was a change in the river's meanderings. The very slow flow belied what was ahead, and as our preparation had not been as good as it should have been, we were not aware of the swing of the main flow, which narrowed to the left side of the river. It could be seen from a way off, so we prepared for the increase in speed, and braced ourselves for the event. We lined the raft beautifully to enter the narrow rapid, but first one of the rear passengers tumbled off backwards, then the other, and finally my fellow front passenger decided to abandon ship. I remained the only crew, unfortunately, the craft was somewhat unbalanced now, causing my good self to be tipped forward into the water, and under the now overturned raft.

Luckily I soon surfaced to find the rest of the crew safe, but wet, and we all made the right bank safely. There were students along the river's course, and our raft was pulled ashore, to be salvaged later, while we all made our way to the road leading to Gwaelod-y-Garth. Fortunately, a farmer was at hand, and he offered to warm us up, and took us to the cowshed where he turned on a hot water hose, and sprayed us down, warming and cleaning us at the same time.

We were then picked up and returned to our start point, before changing and joining in the festivities later. It is a shame that the event no longer takes place, especially as the river is now clean, and teeming with life. The river itself is a great asset to the towns it flows through, but its value does not seem to be appreciated or utilised by the authorities along its path.

A local excursion at the time was a trip to the Paget Rooms in Penarth, where the weekly dance offered an opportunity to meet new girls. A short trip in the green Ford was also a pleasure, even though you never knew when it would let you down. On this occasion, all seemed to be running smoothly, the car had behaved itself, we had parked close to the dance hall, and although there were no conquests that evening, we ended the night to drive home in buoyant mood. I cannot remember who was with me, but we returned to the car for the twelve mile drive home with the usual chat of the night's proceedings. I was driving, and all was well until I turned the headlights on. Nothing; no side-lights, no headlights, no dashboard lights. We checked everything we could under the poor street lights, but no joy. The route home was familiar to me, and the time of day meant there was little traffic, so a strategy was unfolding in my mind to get us home without alerting the law. I would risk the first half mile until I reached an open road, and would then await a suitable surrogate vehicle to follow.

We waited a while, and tried one vehicle, but it was too fast for our old wagon, so we waited again. A slow moving car approached, and I put my foot hard down, and got on his tail. Over Leckwith Hill and down towards Cardiff, close to my leader, he took us half way, before turning off somewhere. Another wait for a surrogate tow, but no luck, and so Plan B: make a run for home, with my oval white wall tyres advertising my approach to any law man on duty.

Happy ending; we made it home; as for the lights, I have no recollection how, or if I ever sorted them, but the wobbly white wall tyres gave endless amusement to many more people while the car was out and about.

September 4th 1965 was to be Derick and Margaret's wedding day. It was the first time for me to have the honour of being best man. Of all the couples I have known, they must be top of the list for the perfect match, along with Len and Ida Hudson from Ynysybwl. It was Len to take the photographs while I did my best-man duties. I was more nervous than at our wedding the year before.

St. Mark's hosted the big day, and we went to the town centre for a reception at Princes restaurant. It was here that I allowed my wicked side to plan a little surprise for the unsuspecting couple. Another friend, Colin was in on the plan, and after a successful reception, we all went our separate ways to prepare for an early start the next day.

We had managed to ascertain their honeymoon destination, on the English South Coast, with a stop overnight at an unknown town en route. Colin, myself, and our wives left early next morning in my mini, and arrived before them at their hotel. We left a package to be delivered to their room, so that it would be there when they arrived. "Something for the weekend, sir". or " Pack o' three". Yes, they were condoms. In addition I enclosed some of their wedding photographs taken the day before. This was successfully achieved, and we retreated to a safe distance to await their arrival. They arrived and were escorted to their room, where the package was duly discovered. By this time we were entrenched in a suitable vantage point, to view the next moves, and it was not long before Margaret was peering through the window, to find the perpetrators of the prank. Eventually, we plucked up enough courage to enter the hotel, and went to their room and knocked the door. A not-too-surprised couple answered, and after a coffee, a chat, and some laughs, we were for-given the intrusion, and we beat a hasty retreat back home.

Around the same time, another trip was undertaken, to witness an historic event. Sir Francis Chichester was returning from his circum-navigation of the world in his yacht. A few of us felt it necessary to give him a bit of a welcome. We joined half the UK population in doing so, and all four of us enjoyed the celebration of an astonishing achievement by an elderly gent of immense character. Roy, Mair, myself and Elaine had witnessed the arrival of a truly great man, after a journey that must have tested all his mental resources. I am sure that subconsciously I had learnt a lot about myself, in merely wit-nessing this feat of stubborn determination, by a man who could have put his feet up, and enjoyed a peaceful existence during his twilight years. It came to light shortly after this journey, that he had been suf-fering a very serious illness, and only survived a short while after. This reinforces his amazing efforts, and puts him very high on my personal list of great people.

I was never aware of events affecting the way I behaved at the time, but on reflection, I am sure this, and many other events and encoun-ters, had a profound influence on the way I would see myself, and the world around me.

My business was trundling along, and just beginning to diversify, as I was getting asked to attend more and more weddings. This was just as well, as the processing of black & white films was beginning a decline, as colour processing became more popular. Unfortunately, I was not in a financial position to enter that market yet, and as a consequence, had to rely on sub-contracting all this work, giving me a very small financial reward. This fact was to be crucial when the switch to colour became dominant in my particular choice of trade.

In the meantime, I was doing more and more weddings, and as it was in addition to the processing and printing, I was frequently rushing from one to the other. This created a problem or two. I was due to do a wedding one Saturday, and I had very little time between the darkroom work in the morning, and the mid-day wedding. I went straight from the one to the other without changing, and was coping quite well, organising the groups, and progressing towards an appar-ently successful set of shots at the Church, namely St. David's Gelliwastad Road.

While I was organising one particular group, I happened to over-hear one of the guests chatting, and unfortunately, or fortunately, heard a comment, "Pity the photographer looks a bit like a tramp." I remember feeling quite hurt at that precise minute, but when I stood back, I realised there was a lesson to be learnt, and I did. From then on, I was determined never to attend any function, without care and attention to the way I looked. And so, a big thank you to that person, whoever you are.

I am very fortunate to have had such good hearing, throughout my life so far, along with twenty-twenty vision that is still in reasonable order today. Looking back on my chosen profession, it is just as well. I am quite sure that it has been a major influence in any successes I have ever had in my field. It was always taken for granted, and it is a shame that these simple truths are frequently not appreciated by youth. This also applies to health, where simple pains experienced in your youth, are exaggerated out of all proportion, and the general fitness of the young body, is frequently taken for granted.

This brings me to a particular experience I had as a youth, complaining of some simple pain or other, I attended the surgery of my doctor, Dr A Edwards. To explain, he was an avid collector of cameras, and I had some jealousy of his collection, which was well known to many. As he knew me quite well through my parents, he was aware of my new profession, and whenever he saw me, in or out of the surgery, he would immediately up-date me on his latest acquisition, and want to talk about photography. Along with his hearing deficiency, it became difficult to get to the point of my attending the surgery, and on this occasion, I managed to get to the point, and explained a particular problem I had with my lower leg, where I had had pain for some time; he looked, paused, looked at his own leg, and exclaimed; "I have the same problem, and I haven't a clue what it is". He then reverted to explain the intricacies of the new Contax Camera he had procured, without pausing for breath. He was a fascinating man, highly thought of, and rightly so, and I here have to admit, that his reaction at the time, is now understood more clearly, as my young body would heal that minor disturbance on its own, and required no treatment.

As I left the surgery on Gelliwastad Road, I felt disappointed I had received no sympathy or medication, all of which must have taught me some kind of lesson, as I remember the incident so clearly.

Politics

My interest in politics that erupted around then, is still an enigma to me, as I really do not know how or why it started. As I mentioned, the Young Liberals was more a social thing, but must have had an influence. I seem to get involved with many things at the same time, and this was no exception. I briefly became the Chairman of the Welsh Young Liberals, was about to become a father for the first time, and the business was approaching a critical period that would need a lot of my attention.

What did I do? I decided to stand in the local elections for the then Pontypridd Urban District Council. Something would have to give, and in due course it did, but not before I achieved some measure of success. May 1966 was to be my baptism in the electoral arena, along with a small group of very dedicated candidates and helpers, we set about the task in earnest, trying to upset the equilibrium of the ruling group, the Labour Party.

The leader of our group was a most formidable lady, Mrs Mary Murphy. She was already a councillor, and had already ruffled a few feathers locally and through South Wales. Others in the mix of candidates and helpers, were Reg Green, Mr Davies of Rhydefelin, and a host of the YLs, all committed to upsetting a few of the establishment, who had had it their own way for so long unopposed.

I came to the scene very close to the final date for enrolment as a candidate, and the small group already had candidates in several wards in the town, spreading the helpers very thin on the ground. I was living at the time in the Rhondda Ward, but worked in the Town Ward, and had far more contacts in the Town area, so decided to stand there, especially as there was no contest in that particular ward. I had made the decision to stand, and it was understood from the outset, that I could not expect much help from the group, as they were needed in the crucial wards, where there was a real chance of a win. I dived headlong into the fray with all the exuberance of a lemming taking a leap into the unknown.

My opponent was a gent from the Graigwen area, a short pleasant man whose name eludes me. He was, as most in his party were, confident that history would automatically re-elect any from his party, which had been in almost complete, and unopposed control for decades. As I write this, the feelings of the moment are returning, and I see clearly that it was the rebel in me that said, fight this monopoly, and shake things up.

I set about writing leaflets, and planning my strategy for ruffling a few more feathers, allowing most other parts of life to go on hold. The ward was well spread, and geographically, split in two, with the more affluent Town area the most likely vote friendly, and so, being the rebel, I started in the council estate of Glyncoch. Doing most of the delivering of leaflets myself, I got to meet so many great people that I would never have met otherwise, and I will never regret the paths I took on my attempts to win a seat in that bastion of Labour controlled Councils.

Strangely, a few of the names I remember from this period, were the opposition guys, in particular Mr Stone, John Cheesman, Charlie Anzani, George Paget, Mr. Bowden and an amazing array of faces, clearly etched into my memory, sadly without names attached. It is a simple truth, that many a confrontation at one time, will lead to a friendship at another; and it is a shame that we all could not have such foresight when we are young.

A storm began to brew a day before the election, I had put out a second leaflet to the Glyncoch Estate the day before the Election, and it was deemed to be a "dirty trick" by the opposition. It soon became obvious that it was a touch of panic setting in, when the possibility of a close contest was on the cards. The leaflet does not exist any more, but the crux of it was an attack on the way the estate had been planned and built, without any green play areas, but simply a policy of start building houses in one area, and simply keep going until the area was full.

It struck home in many hearts, and had I pushed this observation earlier it may well have been decisive. However, on the day, we made a massive impact on an Estate that had seemed impregnable, and had sown a seed that could bear fruit at some future date. This was illustrated, by one gentleman that I met on a canvassing trip. He was a lifelong member of the opposition, but had clearly shown a sympathy for my opinions, and on the day of the election, he put my poster in a very prominent position in his window. This may seem insignificant in today's climate, but it was a serious statement in that era, and to my delight he supported us for some years after.

Another incident from early on in the campaign, was a chance meeting with a guy who was determined to let me know, that the only solution for the world's ailments was a Communist State. I remember listening intently, and getting involved in conversation for some time, making absolutely no headway at all. He then informed me that he had successfully delayed me from canvassing for a considerable period, and that would help the Labour candidate. He called me back when I had moved on to the next house, and when I reached his front door he secretly whispered, that I had convinced him, and that I would get his vote, but I had to keep it to myself. He further said that it had been the fact that I smiled and listened, that had the greatest influence on his actions, a lesson stored away, that influenced other activities, unrelated, but significant in their end product.

Subsequently I met him, and he openly admitted to supporting my cause, but always maintained he was a Communist. Reflecting on this story, reinforces my present day philosophy, that respect must be a requisite for us all towards our fellow man, if there is to be a better world order for our children.

At the count that evening, there was great excitement in some quarters, and despair in others. In the final analysis, it really doesn't matter too much, as it is the way one reacts to situations that really counts, and on this occasion I came second, but was near enough to cause some heart searching by many of those close to the action. As for me, I returned to working on keeping the family in food and clothing until the next challenge.

Later that year, on November 4th. Donald Campbell launched his boat Bluebird on Lake Coniston, to make a further attempt on the world water speed record. It was the latest of many he had completed over the years, both on water, and on land in his Bluebird car. So many records in his locker, and yet he wanted another. This would be his last, as history tells, but here, I add my tribute to a man with a dedication that is to be greatly admired, for his calm commitment to something almost intangible, a record. People climb mountains because they are there; he was making an assault on his mountaintop because it was there.

Our first baby was due sometime in January, and these next months passed all too swiftly. Little information was being reported for the first weeks of his proposed attempts, but soon the news was that the attempt may never happen, and the pressure was building on Donald Campbell to go for it. He knew that was not a good way to go about such a dangerous attempt, as the conditions had to be perfect for a serious high-speed attempt. Unfortunately, the pressure and the impatience of the media, proved the undoing of this normally patient man.

Early on the morning of the 4th. January, 1967, the weather was fine, and the surface of the lake was like glass, perfect conditions. Preparations were made for an attempt at the record to be made as early as possible. The first run was a fantastic 297mph through the measured mile. So far, so good, but sooner than expected the roar of the engine was heard at the far end of the lake for the return leg. This premature start to the second half of the attempt was to be his down-fall. Not enough time had elapsed for the ripples from the first run to subside. When Campbell's boat reached over 300mph, the unthink-able happened and the boat lifted off, with fatal consequences.

The news was full of these events for days. When our son was born six days later, I suggested Donald as his first name, and it was done and dusted. Thankfully he has never aspired to emulate such speeds, but is no mug in a go-cart. His arrival put a new perspective on life, although I have always felt that I could, and should have done more for him and the future arrivals. If I have felt a failure in anything, it would be fatherhood. In my defence, I suppose I could say, "I did it my way".

The local elections were approaching, and I really fancied another crack at the establishment. This must make it sound like a vendetta, but that would be far from the truth, as I had a strong sense of com-munity spirit, and felt very strongly, that there was huge room for improvement in many areas of local politics.

As I was writing the last paragraph, I had a phone call from Toronto, Canada, from an acquaintance met briefly in Bombay in 1962. He is visiting the UK in September and it is hoped that we can meet again, and renew an old friendship. More of this, with details, a little later in the book.

Back to our new arrival and the progress into parenthood, The draw of the Lake District was strong, and Elaine and I decided to take a trip to renew our association with that lovely part of the country, and visit particularly Coniston Water, where Donald Campbell had so recently lost his life. We drove the 200 plus miles, with our Donald in his brown carry-cot, that also fitted into his pram, and enjoyed a few days taking in the atmosphere of the place, and meeting some of the crew that had supported the Campbell attempt. The then owner of the Sun Hotel, where Campbell had stayed, was happy to relate stories of the visits, and I purchased a framed photograph of one of Campbell's speed attempts along the lake. It is still in my possession, the view of the lake, with the wake of Bluebird stretching way back along the length of the photo, and the craggy, snow-clad 'Old Man' behind the village of Coniston.

Elaine stood the rigours of the journey well, but Don was, of course, oblivious to the experience. We took a small motorboat for a spin around the lake, where my navigation left a bit to be desired. I got wedged on some rocks, when I got too close to shore, but we managed to extricate ourselves eventually. Don and Elaine put up manfully with my silly adventures, but the time spent on the lake that day was more of a spiritual bonding with the unknown. It was rather like closing a door, before walking across the next room of a large mansion.

Before we left Coniston, we came across a violin maker, Fred Smith, I think his name was, and a visit to his home and workshop was a revelation. He welcomed me, and offered to show me around, even though I wasn't a musician, but just an interested onlooker. I have never been an avid DIY man, but his collection of specialist chisels and tools of all descriptions was mightily impressive, more so as he had made many if not all himself. He was very well known, then, but his demeanour was one of a humble man, with no semblance of conceit or arrogance. I immediately took to his obvious passion for his work and his openness in sharing his passions with his fellow man. The fiddles in the middle of manufacture, were all around, some varnished, some in a skeleton stage, but with a beauty all their own. He only had enough special wood left to make one or two more instruments, as the special wood was no longer available. Some years later, I saw an interview on TV with Yehudi Menuhin and him, discussing the instruments, one of which was purchased by Yehudi for £500. If I have got any details wrong, I apologise here, but I do not think I am far out.

Back home to try to keep the business going, and start the canvassing for the May elections. This time, I was up against a local headmaster, and I prepared a first leaflet on similar lines to the final one of the previous year's election. It was obvious that I was being taken more seriously than before, as the criticisms came my way one after the other. The fact that I lived just outside the Ward, and my tender years (27), my hippy-type appearance with the full bushy beard, gave them ample scope for their remarks. I was enjoying myself too much to worry about such remarks, and I continued the canvassing, especially in the Glyncoch part of the Ward.

By now, I had several helpers, with Ian and John taking some of the load off my shoulders, as well as Jean and Ashley, and it went more or less to plan, with our constant house visits to put our point of view over to the voters.

When the polls closed that night, I was just a little excited, although not at all sure of the outcome. I picked up one of my helpers from the polling booth in Glyncoch, and started the drive to the Municipal Buildings where the count would take place. I drove in my usual brisk fashion, chatting away to my passenger as we sped along Garth Avenue, reaching the junction of Cefn Lane. With a quick glance at the relevant traffic, I pulled out. Schreeeeeech; I had not seen a vehicle coming up the road, luckily we avoided a collision, but my lady passenger took a little time to recover.

At the count, we met up with all the other candidates, and compared notes on our hopes for success. We were fighting several Wards, and we were hopeful of gaining some ground, although my prospects were not too promising. It became obvious that we were winning in one or two Wards, but in all honesty, I could not tell how my particular count was going. But as the end of the count drew nearer, I could barely believe what I was seeing. The piles of votes for me were considerably higher than my opponent, and it was confirmed that I had pulled off a major victory. The moment was only dented slightly by the refusal of my opponent to shake hands, and the sheer joy of success lasted all of 24 hours. Then the realisation of the hard work that would ensue; and the cost to me, and my family, financially, mentally, and physically. It was like going over the top, the initial adrenalin rush, followed by the realisation of what you had let yourself in for. I will never regret the adventure, but mentally, I was just not prepared for the tensions and the demands made on all councillors. They are often vilified by people who often have no concept of efforts put in on their behalf, especially in those early days, when it cost the councillors hard cash to do their job properly, at least if you were gainfully employed.

A footnote to these proceedings, is that the opponent I had beaten with a large majority, became a friend, not politically, but through a school he was associated with. And although he is no longer with us, I admit that I learned a lot through the experience of working around him. I also learned a lot about people, through my work in the Council chamber, much of it not easy to accept, as I was on the wrong side to get any benefit, but on the side to be trodden on at every opportunity. I can only remember a couple of instances when I felt I had achieved anything. The allocation of houses to one of your ward applicants, was generally up to the three ward members to decide, and after my first year, I had been joined by another Liberal, giving us a majority in our Ward. John Edwards and I were then able to be our own judge of an applicant's needs, so we were actually in a position to make a difference.

In the last year of my three-year stint, I made a concerted effort to correct an anomaly that I felt quite strongly about. I had tried on two occasions previously, to introduce a motion, to change the rule of NOT opening the Ynysangharad Park sports facilities on a Sunday. This was a throw back to the non-conformist churches in Wales, and I felt this was completely inappropriate in that age. My first attempt was not even supported by my five colleagues, and the vote was 26 to one. On the second introduction of the same proposal, it was 20 to seven. In that final year, I was amazed to see a proposal put forward by the Labour group, for the same change. You guessed it, it passed by 27 to 0 and they claimed the credit. I am unable to show you a picture of my expressions at that debate, but I leave it to your imagination. The facilities have been fully used on Sundays ever since.

During this era, we had moved to 2, Bridge Buildings, Pwllgwaun, situated at the Ponty end of the Rhondda ward, adjacent to the river Rhondda. We had been helped with the deposit to buy the property, by my uncle in Birmingham, who had been more than generous, and had given us a start on the property ladder. It had been a corner shop previously, and was somewhat run down, but we managed to get the shop into some sort of workable shape, and opened as a sweet shop, while advertising my photographic work.

In the meantime we had acquired an addition to the family, namely Poldenhills Symphony Chinchilla, a daughter of the famous Cosset Carpet Cat, Merlin. We had travelled to Berkshire to collect the beautiful animal, as a surprise for Elaine. The cat was a revelation, and probably, no, definitely, the loveliest animal ever. She would sit on the back of Elaine's chair and lick her hair, she would come to you when she was called, and at bed time, we would open the door at the bottom of the stairs, and say "up to bed" and she would trot up to her special sleeping place, like a dutiful child.

She was a house cat, and her large melting eyes, would melt any heart that saw her, and the only time she ventured out, would be with us in the car. On one such occasion, we were on our way to a friend's house, and called into Taff Street, Pontypridd to buy something. We stopped when I saw one of my relatives to chat, and wound down the window just a little to talk. Whoooosh, out went Symphony and under a parked car. The panic that ensued, would make one think that our last pound had fallen down a drain, and it took several of us to recapture our terrified new sibling from the traffic ridden main street.

The basement became my darkroom and workshop, where I continued the black & white processing and printing service for the local chemists. This side of the trade was now in serious decline, and I looked more and more to weddings and general commercial work to make a living. The one thing about the basement that sticks in my mind, was the earth floor, even in the work area, there were only a few flagstones. When I pass the now derelict property, I often have the urge to try and get in for a look around. Such negativity lasts but a moment or two now, as it is tomorrow that is important to me.

Looking at the position of this property, it is surprising that we never had any flooding, when just a short distance up the valley, at Trehafod, there were a few instances of very serious flooding. I received a call from someone local who knew I was a councillor, asking for assistance. I got in touch with the council department, and set off the short distance to the scene of the flooding. The wellington boots were soon wet inside and out, as the River Rhondda's muddy waters surged over the banks and through the row of terraced houses on Rhondda Road. By the time I got there, the residents were desperately trying to save some of their belongings, as the dirty water settled waist high on the ground floor. As they saved what they could, in the confusion of the situation, none of us noticed that the electrics were still on, and in a moment of reaction, I said "we need to turn off at the mains". In the hallway I noticed the metal fuse boxes, with the metal on-off lever, and without stopping to think, I reached up, still up to my waist in water, and pushed the metal lever to off. Everything went dark, and a sudden realisation swept over me. I could so easily have been electrocuted, as I was standing in water. Maybe another cat-life was used up there.

The houses are long gone now, and the road widened to accommodate the dreaded car, and flood defences have improved the area generally. Yet whenever I pass the spot, the memory of the night still surges through the mind, rather like the river surged through the houses.

I must here pay a personal tribute to a friend who saved me from the ignominy of being declared bankrupt. Bruno Bertorelli had been a friend for many years, and we often chatted over coffee or a meal, either at his home in Tyfica Road, or in his café in Taff Street. My business was close to his, and lunch was usually obtained there. The firm that had been giving me a service, processing and printing the colour work, were pressing for a full payment of their monthly bills.

Because of the decline of the black & white market, I had been unable to keep up with their bills. I had been hiding the facts from myself, let alone others, but somehow friends know when something is wrong, and so it was with Bruno.

Another contributory factor to this financial imbalance was the fact that when I became a councillor, I mysteriously lost all my contracts with the schools, where I gave annual sets of groups and individual photographs of the students. I was informed by the Labour controlled County Council, that they were setting up their own department to undertake this work, and that private firms would no longer be permitted to do it. One week later a firm (private) in Cardiff took over all my school work. No comment!

I had a phone call one evening, and a very soft tone voice asked, "how much do you need?". I was flabbergasted, and asked who it was and how he knew. He said he had guessed, and it did not matter how, and again asked how much I needed. I eventually went to see him, and he agreed to pay off the debt, and I agreed to pay him back as soon as possible. Words cannot describe the relief and gratitude I felt. It made our friendship even stronger. I am still good friends with his family, although he passed on many years ago.

All these financial difficulties, along with the pressures of being a councillor, made it difficult to tell which was the trigger for the breakdown that was on the horizon. Business was at a low ebb, and I decided to supplement our income by taking an additional job, so I applied for one with the Rhondda Bus Company as a conductor. I duly completed the necessary training, and was soon operating services up and down the Rhondda Fach, and the Rhondda Fawr, as well as to Talbot Green and Porthcawl.

This was in addition to the photographic work, which was mostly on weekends. This put huge strain on Elaine, who coped really well, especially as we were expecting our second child. Helga was born on September 6th, at home, with me assisting a great Indian doctor at the delivery. I know that gas and air was used, but by whom, I don't remember. Helga is another special person to grace this planet of ours.

Here I have to admit to a blurring of the years from 1967 to 1970; and although many separate episodes are clear, I cannot put them in chronological order. One event that sticks strong in the brain, is the day I went to work very early one morning, and started on a single deck bus, dispensing tickets as usual. As the day progressed, I became more and more agitated, and when I got to the depot in Porth to take on my next run, I was on a double deck bus. That was the final straw that set off a panic attack that left me clinging to the bar on the platform, unable to move, let alone go to the upper deck. I was taken off the bus, and it was the last action of that short period of employment. Still today I have a fear of upper decks of buses, and remember the sinister effect this incident had on me. The world literally went grey, and I recall being at home, sitting, and feeling like an empty eggshell. I went through the motions of living the next few days, until one morning, I descended the stairs to the living room in floods of tears, that simply went on and on. The grey of the surroundings is what sticks in my mind, for it was as though the world had become black & white.

I was admitted to hospital at East Glamorgan Church Village, where I stayed for six long weeks, and it made me understand how a person can easily become institutionalised. I have one lasting memory of a feeling that has never returned. It was a strong notion that I was a failure, to my wife, my children, and mostly to myself, and I have a strong suspicion, that much of what I had seen and experienced in India, was beginning to get a hold of 'Self'.

One event that may have started the process of recovery, was a bad day on the ward, when I was very agitated, and really needed a shoulder to lean on. There was none, and I was pushing the staff one step too far. The consequences were swift, painful and, I remember, very frightening. I have since discovered that I was given a tranquilliser injection, that, I am sure, would have put a rhino to sleep, and it took some time for me to recover. When I did, I had a bed surrounded by medics. One of the nurses told me much later, that there had been some concerns over my condition. For me though, the most difficult consequence of the whole episode was the fear of going out of the hospital building. After one or two short walks, the feelings faded away, and, I trust, will never return.

While all these events were floating along, the family support had stayed strong, and my brother, Bryan, who was now resident in South Africa, had offered to fund a trip to Port Elizabeth where he was involved with a scheme he thought would suit me. After my release from hospital, I had little work, and we decided that it was worth a try, and if the prospects looked good, Elaine and the children could follow.

The last act in the hospital was played out in the psychiatrist's office, after I had requested a consultation. I told him I wanted to get through this thing on my own, without the dreaded pills if possible, to which he said, "that's what I have been waiting for you to say", and that really, was that. The pockets full of awful drugs, and a strong desire to put the episode behind me, I tried to get back to a positive mode, and returned home to prepare for South Africa.

A month or so later, I was on my way, although still taking these pills. I am sure they blocked large tracts from my memory, as the only strong images start a week or so after my arrival in Port Elizabeth. My eldest brother Bill and his family were well established there, and lived in a well-appointed area in one of the suburbs, while Bryan had a small flat nearer town. I stayed here for the duration, and recall my surprise at the helpers he had to cook and clean every day. They were the most charming ladies that reminded me of characters in old films like *Gone with the Wind*. They were happy, smiling and uncomplaining, but I felt an underlying unease in their demeanour.

Apartheid was, of course, in full swing in that era, and I was soon to be confronted with the full meaning of the word. In the meantime, I got to know the layout of the place, and do have a few pleasant pictures of the walks I made around the neighbourhood. It seemed completely safe; rather like back home, but with dirt roads and not tarmac. The one thing that took my eye, was the roofs of almost all dwellings; painted greens, reds and blues, and made of corrugated metal. I do not recall any slate or tiled roofs, and on a visit decades later, it seemed this had not changed much.

Bryan had arranged for me to attend a seminar, and I was suitably impressed by the first impressions. It was an American organisation that Bryan was involved in, and where he claimed to have made a lot of money. I went in with an open mind, but soon saw chinks in the armour of the slick presenters of the concept. With hindsight, it was obvious, but the enthusiasm of the tutors was catching, and we were swept along in a flood of excitement, at the prospects they were proposing. One day, about two or three days into the course, I suddenly twigged where we were going, and knew it would not be where I was going.

I put this down to an incident a day after I had arrived. I woke one morning to find Bryan gone off to work, and was alone in the flat. I had breakfast and went to take the dreaded pills allocated to me, and paused; why am I taking these things? I was sure, very suddenly, that they had to go, and I flushed the lot down the toilet. It was an instinctive move, made with complete confidence in myself, and I am sure it was a result of much of the advice and support I had received from family, and the hospital. I am not sure it is the right thing to do in all situations, but it was right for me at that time, and in that place.

The course was designed to enrol people into Pyramid Selling.

Their product was very good, a full complement of cosmetics, with names like cucumber facial creams, and strawberry tonic cleansers. It was the method of selling that was the new concept, and I saw very quickly, that there were flaws in the idea, especially for me, only recently arrived in a new country. Bryan, however, was involved from a very early stage, and had already made a lot of money; but it could not be maintained, and subsequently, that proved to be the case, and months later, he lost much of his earlier gains.

Strangely though, I gained a great deal from the course, with Positive Thinking a strong theme throughout. I remember very clearly at the end of the week-long course, a one-to-one interview with one of the tutors, who asked me why I was rejecting the idea. My reply was on the lines of, "If you sing a note for long enough, it will begin to fade", and I explained that I could not see how anyone except the people at the top could succeed. The entire concept was eventually banned in many countries, and South Africa was one of them.

I was, by the end of the week, feeling very strong and single minded, and was already planning what I would do on my return to the Valleys. I intended to set targets for the business, and would concentrate on future market progress, working towards financial success. Part of this I saw through, and part I rejected, and whether I had already started to think in terms of rejecting personal materialism, or was taking cognisance of the volatile situation there in South Africa, I may never know. The end product was that I would return home, and restart my photographic business, and would definitely not get involved in Pyramid Selling.

Before returning home, I spent a little time in Port Elizabeth, visiting my oldest brother and his lovely family, and finding a strong pro-Apartheid feeling throughout, something I found completely unacceptable. This difference of opinion certainly affected future relations. An incident that occurred some time during my attendance at the course, was to be a catalyst for my thinking. I had waited for the lift to go to the fourth floor, and was joined by a young black boy. We chatted, as I usually do, and as we waited, were joined by a rather large white South African Boer. When the lift arrived, he pushed the boy aside, and stepped into the lift, ushering me in also. I declined his offer, put my hand on the black boy's shoulder, and said, "I will wait for the next lift with my friend". He went up alone.

The feeling that incident left with me has lasted, intact, ever since. Throughout my visit there, I was aware of the divisions in society that went far beyond anything I had ever witnessed before. It was not just blacks and whites, but more poignantly between whites and whites, and I remember an unease of mind for years after.

Towards the end of my stay, I had been interested to speak to lots of the locals wherever I met them, and thought nothing of chatting to a couple of young ladies I had met, who had been on the same course as me. We were on the main shopping street of P.E. and after a while my brother Bryan appeared, and very abruptly ushered me away. Later he told me that it was inadvisable to openly chat to any coloured or black, as the police could take a dim view of it, and could even arrest me for such a crime.

That all seems strange to me now, but it showed the underlying fears that existed in those dark days while Mandela was still incarcerated, although at that juncture, I was unaware that he existed.

Bryan was most understanding of my decision to return home, although he was still convinced of the project's potential, but it was not too long after I left, that the whole idea was outlawed. He was, however, a most resourceful character, and soon found a way to open some new doors, and became a successful salesman and fitter of vertical blinds.

Something that came to light much later, was that Bryan had been involved in a multi-cultural project to promote a mixed shopping complex, that had made him a target for the same reason he had warned me about. I never found out how his involvement ended, but one can only speculate, considering the volatile nature of the society he was living in.

I must here pay tribute to Bryan's sportsmanship, which continued throughout his life. His great passion was bowls; a sport that had dominated his life in P.E. He spoke to me at length on his final visit to the UK, and revealed his passion for the sport, that had originally been a substitute for his retirement from golf. Bryan had been an international table tennis player for Wales, and was well known for his all round sporting prowess. As a young man he had won five consecutive club championships at Pontypridd Golf Club, and there is still in existence, a short piece of film of one of these events. Bryan had assured me, that he was about to start a book, on his approach to sport, but sadly, he never did.

Back to Butlins

Back home to 2, Bridge Buildings, and a renewed vigour to get my photography up to speed and evolving into new areas. This came sooner than I had expected, when the opportunity arose for an additional job in the weekdays, as the Press photographer at Butlins Barry. Most of my work had been on Saturdays, and it seemed a great way of doubling my income, without jeopardising my business. So it turned out to be, although it put great strain on our marriage, as the hours were horrendous. I would frequently drive back and forth to Barry twice a day, in a car that had seen better days, and to compound the issue, I took on an extra task of making the Butlins Movie News, which was a weekly film of the activities on camp.

Still not completely over my bout in hospital, I was advised by the photographic manager, Mr Peter Wilson, that both tasks would be a tall order, but gave me a chance to prove myself. It turned out to be good for us both, and we have maintained a friendship ever since, more recently in the local jazz scene, but still with help to each other in the photographic field.

I had by now acquired more suitable cameras for the work I wanted to do, and along with this, a growing knowledge of filmmaking. Having been an avid 8mm film-maker as a teenager, I fell into the task with an eagerness that made me almost fanatical in my desire to create. The experience proved to be invaluable, although at the time, we had no knowledge of the impending video revolution.

Since I first worked at Butlins in Pwllheli, the still camera equipment had improved, along with the flash equipment, but the cine camera was an ex-army, triple-turret, Bell and Howell, which had been standard issue during the Second World War. It was very robust, and I am sure would save me from mortal injury if ever shot at. The hand winding mechanism was great for building arm muscle power, and the motor like a silenced machine-gun; but the fun of using such a machine is indescribable.

My job with regard to the movie-news, was to start filming on Sunday morning, capturing a flavour of the competitions, and the campers enjoying themselves. The Holliday Princess, Glamorous Granny, Knobbly Knees and many more, were dotted along each day, and I would process the 100 foot films, usually seven per week, and edit and splice them together, along with a few comedy sections that had been filmed early in the season. All this, as well as the press photos that was a job on its own, would keep me out of mischief most of the time.

The film was of course, silent, so the chief Redcoat would always do a commentary on the film in the Theatre. As an opener, I had put together an intro scene, that showed the said Redcoat asleep in his chalet. A close up of a bedside clock would show he was late, and him waking to realise this. He leaps out of bed, dresses as he runs down the chalet line, past the Princess Ballroom, gaining speed with a little trick photography, past the pool, and into the Gaiety Theatre. Up the stairs, through the table tennis hall with another trick shot of him almost swallowing a ball, and on up the stairs and into the back of the theatre.

By this time the campers would be watching the film and anticipating the arrival, making some noise. At the appropriate moment, he would crash through the door at the back of the theatre, and run noisily, and out of breath down the aisle to his microphone seat at the front. It never failed, and I can still see the sequence as if my mind had a video implant installed.

Again, I met so many new friends on this job, but unfortunately, it did little for my marriage, especially as at least once a week there was late night cabaret. This meant returning to camp at around 11.30p.m. and not getting home till around 3.00 or 4.00a.m. My job here was to get as many pictures of campers with the stars of the show, and it usually meant staying till very late until the stars would spare a minute or two. Some were more tolerant than others, and I shall only speak of three that were very good, and ignore the less than gracious few.

Top of the list I put Bob Monkhouse; he was the most gracious man, of the stage variety, that I ever encountered, closely followed by Ken Dodd. Both would invite several of those working during their performance, to a drink in their changing room after the performance, and we would talk for hours on a wide variety of subjects. The most notable thing was that they listened, and we talked. Monkhouse seemed so interested in anything that was said, and showed his compassionate side on more than one occasion. Ken Dodd was very similar, and so different to the image he portrayed on stage.

The experience gathered on this job would lead to a very interesting end. Peter Wilson, the head of our department, had recommended me to one of his bosses, to make a documentary in Greece, and near the end of the season, Mr Archbald came to the camp, and asked if I would film a bus-tour to Greece. It was a three-week assignment, travelling with a bunch of tourists, overland to Athens. I accepted, and gave a price that was way under the norm, except I did not know the norm.

The trip was with a bus company from Bishop Stortford, and we started out a week or so after the end of the Butlins season. It was mid-September and here I was, setting off again on a new adventure, along with my newly acquired Pailard Bolex 16mm cine camera. Looking back now, I realise that the task of filming, without any auto-exposure facility, and not any chance to see any results until a week or so after returning, was daunting to say the least.

The training and experience acquired with Butlins was immense, and I seem to recall no thoughts of anything but success, and so it turned out. The few images that remain of this trip are very clear, the first of which was the journey over the Alps. I was dropped off near the summit of one of the hills, and the bus went back about a mile, and then drove back towards me, in order for me to record a scene reminiscent of *The Sound Of Music* images. The most memorable experience of those shots, was under foot, as when I set up the shot, my tripod, along with me, sank into at least six inches of mossy grass. The scene, however, was very successful, and gave a special flavour of the route we were taking.

In Athens, and on several trips they had included, I was required to show everyone partaking of the magnificent scenery, and enjoying the facilities at the various hotels. One evening, I decided to go alone to the Parthenon, and try and get some shots of the sunset over the ruin. To my amazement, the people in charge said I could have a slot, to film after the tourists had left. I must have spent an hour, getting some amazing footage of the Acropolis, and a superb sunset, without a single person on the site. I was even able to take some delayed action shots of myself, with some stunning backdrops.

The camera I used is still part of my collection of old cameras and equipment, and it was still working the last time it saw the light of day. The film was a couple of weeks in preparation, and when complete, I took it to the headquarters of the bus company, and arranged for one of their staff to view the film in advance, in order for them to do a commentary for their clients. All went successfully, and I went home with little money, but some great memories, and a whole lot more experience. The off cuts of the filming are still in a box somewhere, although I no longer have a projector to show 16mm film.

Shortly after this contract, we came to the conclusion that the house in Pwllgwaun was not a viable proposition. It was about then we moved back to 4, Mackintosh Road, with my mum, as the financial problems had meant a complete re-think of our strategy for the next years. I took a job, temporarily, with a crisp and biscuit company, that had a fleet of 3-ton vans delivering to small businesses and schools. It was a salesman's job really, and I think I knew that it would only be a stopgap until I rekindled the business. Unknown to me then, was that it would be a job that would have unforeseen repercussions. The fact that I was working fairly regular hours, was to be the crucial factor.

The job itself was uninspiring, but was ideal for me, giving me breathing space to organise my next move. I soon arranged to rent a shop in Bridge Street opposite the Park, where I was to re-establish myself as a general photographer. I opened with a splash of publicity, asking the Glyncoch Swingers Jazz Band to do the honours, with a march through town, and then to the shop. They were the reigning World Champions at the time, and certainly got things off to a swinging start.

Having completed three or four months with the crisp firm, I reverted to full time photography, mainly doing weddings and home portraits. With only a short break between businesses, it turned out to be hard work getting up to speed, and making enough to live off. But slowly, I re-established the business, adding a new string to my bow, with home baby portraits, that really helped keep things moving, but this and my late night work in the Clubs around the town, were causing tensions at home.

My job style had taken its toll, and it was soon evident, that the tensions of the trips away, and my late night working, would lead to the inevitable marriage break up. And so it was that we parted, and Elaine and our two lovely children, had to cope with the inevitable trauma of all such breakdowns.

I have tried to look objectively at my reactions and attitudes during this difficult year, and I have surprised myself, finding large areas of fault on my part, although it is very difficult to relate these on paper. It was more my frame of mind that was at serious fault, and I have to admit, that I was still a very selfish individual, looking at life with blinkers on. It is obvious to me now, that I had taken none of my discoveries in India to heart.

Pain, at that stage in my life, was both physical and mental, the physical you always felt was transitory, but pride made the mental pain much more serious, as there seemed no end to it. There seems now, to be a reversal of these two types of pain, brought on by simply getting older. The pains slowly become a progressive non-curable fact of life, which our brain seems to adapt so well to, but the mental strains and pains become so much easier with the age related calm of acceptance. Had I taken more notice of the mind-set of my superficial observations in India, perhaps I could have been a better father and husband and developed the 'Self' much sooner.

I feel sure that this period was to be the catalyst for some major changes in my approach to everyday living, with some well-known philosophies a regular thought in my mind. One is: "if a problem can be solved, solve it, and if the problem can not, then do not try." This seems so simple but so effective in developing positive thinking, and it seems so logical that if we clear our minds of the clutter, the brain can focus so much better on the everyday tasks, this is definitely true of the physical, in that, a cluttered table does not allow a clear path to progress.

Enough of philosophical meandering! Back to the daily developments that were slowly, but surely, leading me in the direction of trying to attain some measure of that inner peace which sometimes arrive in the most unexpected ways. The passing of a loved one is, perhaps one of the most common, and so it was with the events about to unfold.

Dad had died a little while before all these happenings, and Mum had been very adventurous, and taken a slow boat to South Africa. It had always been a longing of hers, and we were all delighted to see her get a dream come true. She spent her months there playing bridge, and enjoying the company of my older brothers, who led quite different lives there.

Bryan was the outgoing friendly type, who seemed to make friends wherever he went, but Bill was an enigma to us all. He was a private man, keeping his thoughts very much to himself, and it must sound insensitive of me, but I really did not know him very well. He had settled in South Africa, married and had a family, but still was distant to me, even when he visited the UK some years earlier. Mum's visit should have been a revelation to him, but, sadly, it was at a stage in his life with some unknown traumas going on, and tragedy struck while mum was on the visit. I received a phone call from Bryan, to say that Bill had died in an accident. He had fallen from a bridge to his death in uncertain circumstances. It appears that after leaving his home, putting out the milk tokens for that days deliveries, and appearing to be untroubled, he proceeded to this bridge, where there were reports of a possible meeting with persons unknown, and an open verdict was eventually concluded by the coroner in Port Elizabeth.

The effect on my mum only became apparent when she returned to the UK, as it immediately affected her health, making her various medical complaints much worse. She rallied well, and never complained, continuing her bridge passion, becoming a regular visitor to the Institute on Gelliwastad Road where she was adored by one and all. I pay tribute here, to her tenacity and courage, for the way she held her grief with immense dignity, and her actions certainly made an impression on me that will last a lifetime. I am sure she has had a considerable influence on the changes in me over the ensuing years. Thanks, mum.

Bryan had his own very strong views on the proceedings of those months, but it is an area that I can never re-enter, as I was far removed from all involved to be able to help in any way. Bill's family still live in SA, although contact is now minimal, Bryan, continued his own inimitable life in his chosen location, and did try a return to the UK much later, but more of that will follow.

Back home at mum's home, my family settled into a routine of building the business up, and mum really enjoying the company of Donald and Helga. She had always wanted a girl in the family, and Helga was the apple of her eye. Sorry Donald, but you came second in this race. In my photographic work I had acquired the camera of all cameras, the Hasselblad, and I am sure this acquisition was a big plus for increasing trade, and with the diversity of the work I was now undertaking, things were looking up, at least on the income front.

I had at last learnt to plan more thoroughly for each job, and had developed a routine of preparations especially for weddings. My style was really to give my clients what they wanted, and not what I or anyone else wanted. One of the trademark changes, was my offer of choice of locations for the photographs, with Castle Coch, Ynysangharad Park and more recently, the famous Rockingstone at Pontypridd's Common. All of these and some others, offered a much more restful background for the couple, and enhanced the overall final effect. Another early photo style I adopted, would be the high vantage big group, the normal shot would have been the wide group, with people trying to be seen over shoulders, or kneeling in front. I would frequently climb trees, stand on walls, hang out of reception windows and many more. It was to create a variation, and develop a practical solution for showing faces of all guests. More than these practical changes, I was, belatedly, learning to listen more, and react better to what I was hearing. I was trying to show more and more of the ambience of the day, as opposed to merely recording the faces.

Child portraits at home was one of my services offered, and it proved effective and profitable. With a little help from a psychologist acquaintance, I developed a technique to put the parents and children at ease. The first contact with the child, I soon discovered, was critical, and I had consulted the psychologist on their advice, and any rules that might be helpful. He gave me a short list of dos, and don'ts, that all seem so obvious when read. Some I had always done, but others were of great assistance to me.

Golden rules: eye contact, smile, whisper, move slowly and do not offer them sweets. With the parents, or worse, grandparents, ask them to be as silent as possible, and where possible restrict it to just one person with them. I found that whispering words to the child often got good reactions, and a good end product photo. In addition to these techniques, the complete understanding of the camera functions, and the control of lighting, were a pre-requisite to success. Personally, I generally used the bounce flash technique, which provided a simple, economic and usually satisfactory result, and it is a technique I still use in my new studio, set up only recently, to cater for the increase in demand, partly caused by the arrival of the digital age.

If you can use all white walls and fittings, in a studio, it is much simpler than the use of studio lighting, and considerably cheaper. In the 70s, there was a move towards the special effects, only one of which has lasted; that is the 'Misty', with endless variations, and was used by most photographers in those days, with varying degrees of success. Others, were the 'super-imposed' face in the glass or music score, the candlelight effect and the soft focus, all of which had a very short life, thank goodness.

I have always felt that the most important person at a wedding, the bride, needs the total focus of the photographer, and if you show her in a good light, then you have succeeded. It has grown to be the criteria on which I base my work at all weddings, and I have always prided myself on giving my very best, to every wedding, whether it be a friend or otherwise. The nervousness I used to feel in my early days as a wedding photographer, has subsided; and I really enjoy the challenge of the different situations each wedding presents.

I must relate here, one or two stories about the experiences I have had at some of these events. The first was a local wedding, that at first seemed to be going quite normally, until the bride began her walk down the aisle. The groom must have had a very sudden realisation of the magnitude of the situation, and by the time his intended had arrived by his side, he was in a state of free fall. His sobbing created a stir amongst the congregation, and he was escorted to the vestry in somewhat of a state. Minutes rolled by, and eventually they all took their places and went ahead as though nothing had happened.

On another occasion, I turned up to a wedding of a mature couple, took the usual preliminary shots of the groom and best man, and waited for the bride to arrive. Some minutes elapsed, and we thought little of it, but after ten minutes or so, I saw a look of anxiety on some faces, and suspected they knew something I did not. All the guests were now in the Chapel, and the best man and one of the mums were whispering to each other, and getting more and more agitated as the clock ticked on. It entered my head that it would be quite a scoop if, in fact she did not arrive at all. My camera was very ready for such an eventuality, and I could see shots of distraught relatives on the front pages of the tabloids.

Suddenly a voice cried, "here she comes", and a sigh of relief all round. Short lived though, because the car stopped some 200 yards from the chapel. By now it was 45 minutes beyond the start, and the fact that it was before the mobile phone era, meant no-one really knew why there was such a delay. The minister had been very patient, and I was engrossed in the situation, and was going nowhere.

The best man took full charge of the situation. He walked the 200 yards to inquire the reason for the delay. He spent some time talking through the window of the car, and this prompted the minister to go also. The groom must now have been thinking he may get away with this very close shave.

Back came the two gents, merely to raise their arms in a gesture of, "we do not know". The drama continued for another half hour, with a visit to the car by at least one more guest, but with no inkling of a reason or an outcome. By now, it was one and a half hours after the scheduled start time, and guests had formed in groups, probably taking bets on the eventual outcome. Suddenly, the car started up, and drove up to the entrance, the Bride and giver away got out as though nothing had happened, the guests took their seats, and she got married.

With all the weddings I have done, I usually remember the bride's faces, but hers was indelibly imprinted on me, and I saw the couple a few times in later years and they were a very happy couple. This was not the case with another couple, who married in the May, and had parted in the June, having had a big spend wedding, with all the trimmings.

The following stories I cannot confirm, but one I am fairly sure is correct. A couple married on the Saturday, went on a two-week honeymoon abroad, and came home separated. Another couple are alleged to have tied the knot, arrived at their reception, eaten their meal, and started the speeches, which were then interrupted by the groom, who announced he was going on holiday alone, as he had discovered his new wife, had been having an affair with his best man. He promptly left.

Make up your own mind, is it a story or real, I confess I do not know. One story I do know is true, was the occasion I took a wedding in the church in Llantwit Major, and all went really well, the album was collected a week later, and they seemed pleased with the final result. Two days later, I received a phone call from a very excited groom, saying I had captured a ghost on one of the shots I took at the church. He said it was the image of Saint Catwg, in a window, behind the close up of the bride and groom.

The following day I received a call from a London paper, the *Observer* asking if they could photograph me with the camera I had used to take the photo. I agreed to this free bit of advertising, and was duly photographed with my prized Hasselblad. The said ghost picture appeared the next Sunday, front page, giving me some great advertising. I was guarded in my interview, as I really did not believe it was anything other than a trick of the light.

Subsequently, I went back to the church, and went through the same procedure, with the same settings, and similar lighting conditions, but could not replicate the effect. And so I leave it to individuals to make up their own minds. It is unfortunate that these, and thousands of other negatives were lost in a flood some years later, and I did not keep a copy of the newspaper.

One occasion that I look back on with some amusement, was at a wedding in the centre of Pontypridd, where all seemed normal until a minute or so before the start, the groom had not arrived, and the bride's car was just arriving. She was sent away by one of the ushers, with a suggestion they go around the block. No mobile phones at this time, meant it was out of everyone's control. Bride's mum was obviously upset, and I again had visions of an exclusive. Here comes the bride again, and still no show by the groom and best man. This time I was the bringer of the bad news. The bride turned white, and I remember, was silent. I wondered if she knew something we did not. Off they went on another tour of the area, a little further this time.

On the third attempt, some ten minutes later, the same scenario, and the bride, her mum and several others were getting somewhat agitated. As her car drove off into another lap, with the meter ticking, and her distress level reaching boiling point, a car pulled dangerously across the traffic, and came to a halt beside the church. The back door opened and the groom literally fell out onto the pavement, followed by the best man, barely keeping his feet. He was dishevelled and still obviously very drunk, and several guests gave assistance to try and get him into a fit state to continue. The minister was also involved and there were serious doubts if the groom could see it through. He was in the entrance, about to be escorted to his place, when the bride arrived, who started to recover some colour in her cheeks when she heard the good news.

I did not take any shots during the ceremony, as this church did not allow this, but I did speak to the best man later, and he said he, and the groom sobered instantly when the wedding march started to play. I cannot report on the conversations that took place later, but I imagine they would have been interesting.

I had always enjoyed my work, and counted myself very lucky to have taken this path, and although I have never felt myself to be a gifted photographer, I have learnt to be consistent and honest in my approach. I learnt early on, that maximum knowledge of your subject, will make the job easier, with technique and camera dexterity taking an insignificant role. As I progressed through the years, the simple adage of knowing your subject, and preparing well, were of paramount importance, and I here have to admit, that it took a few years to learn this basic lesson.

I have often seen the so called experts in TV programmes giving out advice on taking good photographs, some good and some not so good. The advice to the happy-snapper, would be different to that of a serious student or would-be professional. The basic principles for the snapper, would be: take a stance that is solid, with feet apart, or lean if possible against a wall, frame the subject taking notice of the background, and always squeeze the shutter button, and NOT press it suddenly, then silently count one before taking the camera from your eye. This applies to analogue and digital equally, and all the basic principles of the one, equally apply to the other.

As for the serious photographer, I am reluctant to give too many of the lessons I have learnt over the years. The only thing I would say, is that the most important aspect of the job, like most jobs, is to be prepared for any possible eventuality, as this particular profession is subject to last minute changes on a regular basis. Weddings especially are subject to frequent last minute adjustments, and for what it's worth, I have learnt not to fight frantically to follow a plan, but to generally go with the flow, adjusting as I go. This must sound like a contradiction, but where you can follow a plan through, do so, but never close your mind to betterment.

If there is one single word that has transformed situations, on a regular basis for me, it is SMILE. A simple action that can turn a situation in an instant, and I have applied this in so many ways, to so many subjects over the more recent years.

Just maybe, if I had learnt the lesson sooner, the break up of my first marriage would not have occurred. However, the parting was upon us, and it is history. Ifs and buts are irrelevant, the fact is; and the hurt that radiates from such partings is inevitable, with the hurt radiating out to so many third parties. Acceptance is the only eventual salvation, and time is the only healer, although a positive and non-judgemental attitude helps.

At Pontypridd Rugby Club, the supporters' club team had played the odd friendly game, leading to some suggestions of a short holiday on a boat on the Thames. We were eventually five in total, casting off from Oxford, taking in Abingdon, Reading, Windsor and Staines. Yet again I have to admit to having only a sketchy memory of this adventure, but a chance meeting with a member of the crew from the time, recollected some details of the event. Gerald Crocker was one of the intrepid sea-dogs, along with Dai Boyce, Mike Watkins, John Goldsworthy and one other whose name has filtered through the brain banks.

Many a watering hole was visited alongside the banks of the rivers and canals we traversed, leading to some unsteady sea-legs the following day. As the only non-drinker of the party, I acquired the task of steering the boat on many occasions, but on one morning, it was left to Dai to manoeuvre the long boat towards the next lock. We were moving past a number of large expensive craft, moored along the way, with some well to do owners enjoying the peaceful calm of the day on deck. Dai was not really switched on, and drifted rather close to the said craft, realising too late the inevitable consequence of his late reaction to the situation. Much to the dismay of the one particular lady aboard her craft, we gently collided with her boat, luckily getting one of the buffer gadgets between the two craft, avoiding any damage.

We approached a lock with an accompanying pub alongside, deciding to moor the boat and have some lunch. The following story does not register in my memory, but I am assured it did happen, related here by Gerald. A foreign visitor was on a similar holiday to us with his family, and also decided to partake of the pub's hospitality. After a short time there was frantic activity outside, turning out to involve the boat of our visitor, (an Australian I believe).

It turned out he had moored in the lock, so as the water level dropped, so did his boat, slowly but surely leaving his boat dangling from the mooring rope. I wish I could remember the scene, unfortunately it is all a blank for me. My imagination can, however, conjure up the scenario, flowering it into a full length silent movie. This you will have to imagine yourselves as my imagination is mine alone. This last sentence illustrates the way my thinking has changed, in that we all see life the way WE see it, often finding great difficulty seeing the other person's point of view.

Back to the boats, specifically to an evening spent moored somewhere on the banks of either the Thames, the Kennet, or some canal in the area. Again, I only recall a little of this episode as it was again Gerald who reminded me of the incident. For some silly reason, there had been a challenge put, as to who would streak along the banks beside our moorings. I have no doubt that the odd drink had been involved somewhere along the line, a faint memory of a card game, along with rainy weather conditions.

Shamelessly, apparently, I was the first to display my matchstick body to the elements and the world, photos of which I am told still exist. My exploits were followed by others, but I cannot here reveal the full list of participants. The rest, as they say, is history; for me in this instant, a blank history, as I recall nothing else from the trip.

Early one morning I received a strange phone call: "take your cameras, and travel towards Merthyr", that was all, and then rang off. It was October 21st. 1966, around 9.30am. I did not think twice, as it seemed serious, and so it turned out to be. Aberfan is eight miles north of Pontypridd, and long before I got near, it was obvious that there had been a major incident. I swiftly parked a little way off, and walked the three to four hundred yards. The sight that greeted me was one of a strange calm, the only thing I could relate it to, would be standing in the eye of a hurricane.

As I approached the scene, a young boy of around nine or ten sauntered towards me, hands in pockets, head slumped, but no apparent realisation of the enormity of what had happened. He paused, and I said something about the school, he replied quite calmly, almost with pride, that he had been, "late for school". I often wonder where that young man is today, and if the mental scars of that dark day have subsided.

I had arrived with my cameras, but very soon decided to leave them in a local's house, in order to help with any digging work. It seemed to me that taking photographs at a time like this, was inappropriate, unlike the hardened press boys and the paparazzi. Before finding somewhere to lend a helping hand, I briefly watched some miners from the local coal mine, burrowing under the still moving slurry from the tip, putting their lives at risk to try and find survivors.

Even when the gravity of the situation became clearer, there was still the calm amongst the frantic attempts to save lives. In all my life, I have never witnessed a feeling of oneness, as I did on that day, and through the night. I saw bravery to match any, before or since, along with the camaraderie, and total togetherness to compare to the darkest days of the war. The clear image I retain is one of lines of men, women, miners, police, along with, it seemed, the entire population of that small village, all digging furiously in silence, weeping and praying for some miracle. Every few minutes, a whistle would blow, and all would stop, listening for the sound that never came. There were to be no miracles, for all were lost in that black porridge of the slag-heap that had descended that morning.

While we all toiled, we thought only of the work. It was only when exhausted, and we were making our way home, that the enormity of what had happened struck home. I remember walking away from the village towards my car, when emotion flooded over me like an avalanche, and I wept as I passed house after house, doors open, with stunned faces peering into the night. As I approached a working men's club, I was ushered inside and handed a brandy. No charge, they said, and my body slumped into a chair to take a short break. My face black, hands dirty and my clothes in a state, did not matter, it was of no concern at such a moment. Refusing further offers of food and drink, I went on my way, wondering how the families would cope. With my cameras tucked away in the gadget bag, without any photographs having been taken, I got home shortly before dawn, and slept for most of the following day.

5.55pm, a day with little to identify it from any other, then BANG, a loud explosion shook the building. It came from the end of Taff Street, some 100 yards from my shop. I had just taken a passport picture for a customer, and still had the old Pentax S.P. 500 in my hands. I raced the 100 yards to the end of the street to find a large van stationary just outside the Historical Museum, and just short of the famous Old Bridge. It had the roof ripped off and many red and blue LPG gas bottles stacked on the now open backed van. Many bottles were strewn behind the van on the road, which explained the ferocity of the explosion.

I took a couple of pictures of the scene, which at that moment seemed innocuous, but then noticed a very small flame emanating from one of the gas bottles still on the damaged van. Adjacent to this scene was the Kwik-Save Store, so I rushed in and asked if they had a fire extinguisher for me to put out the very small flame. They refused, explaining it was company policy not to allow any use other than a fire on the premises. I returned to take more pictures, and witnessed a man running towards the Police Station some 50 yards away, he leapt over the railings and disappeared inside.

I later discovered that he had announced to the receptionist that the first explosion was just one bottle, that there were 99 more on the van, and there was a fire on board. I did not witness the scene in the offices, but was reliably informed later, that there was a little panic by some of the office staff.

I had used up the couple of shots I had in the camera, so I rushed back to reload in my shop, to capture any possible outcome. When I returned, just minutes later, the small fire from one of the bottles was intensifying, and there were two policemen urgently making the situation as safe as possible. Traffic was stopped, and pedestrians were eventually held way back, waiting for the fire service to arrive.

I was in the middle of the road, some 100 yards from the incident, happily waiting for some drama to unfold, camera at the ready, with a fast shutter speed ready to record any eventuality. I was joined, briefly, by a gent, holding a Practica camera. He asked me what settings to use in these light conditions. Before I could reply, BANG, another bottle exploded, and I got two shots of that particular occurrence. Looking round, there was no sign of the other would-be photographer. I guess he was late for his tea.

After that second explosion there was increased urgency by the police officers on the scene. I was told in no uncertain manner to get well away. No chance, I was not going to miss an opportunity like this, so I went around back of the bus station café, and took up a vantage point behind a low wall. Resting the camera on the wall for stability, I waited for the next explosions. I did not have to wait long. There were upwards of fifteen explosions, the smaller blue bottles giving more of a bang, while the larger red bottles let off a softer bang with more flames.

The fire brigade were fearless in their work to contain the flames. Each explosion created a ball of flame and black smoke, with the canisters hurled hundreds of yards in all directions. I have to admit to being very excited by the whole event. It was just like a mock battle, each bang shaking the ground and the wall I was using as a tripod. The resulting photographs were affected by this vibration, but there were enough good shots to warrant considerable interest from the media.

Only one injury resulted from this accident. A fireman broke a finger when he fell backwards after one of the explosions, his fall caught on one of my photographs, only discovered much later.

As soon as I had photographed the aftermath of the accident, I set about contacting the media to sell the exclusive shots I had been fortunate enough to get. I processed the films, and half an hour after that, had the prints ready. Today, with a digital camera or mobile phone in every pocket, I wouldn't have had a chance of such an exclusive.

Both BBC and ITV took a selection of my shots, with the news full of the images in double quick time. The press also gave me front page coverage, but the most interest came shortly after, when all the big petrol internationals wanted full sets of the take, as it was the first time anyone had captured an incident from before, during and after, illustrating the dangers of carrying LPG bottles.

With hindsight, I should have employed a News Agency to distribute the pictures. As it was, I trusted the media to pay the going rate for such stories. I lost out on a big pay-day, but it really did not and has not since bothered me , as I have never been one for making money, only sufficient for my needs.

I still occasionally get requests for the photographs, keeping samples at my shop, along with an enlargement as an interest photo on display. This brings me to something aluded to earlier in the book, namely, the amateur/professional relationship in business. Since I first started in the trade with Ivor Alderson, there has always been a conflict between the two, and I recall some strong opinions expressed from both sides, regarding non-professionals taking paid jobs such as weddings. As an early observer, I witnessed some strained relationships, where friendships were compromised, and sometimes broken. This situation continues today, especially with the advent of the digital age, where imaging can take place at the drop of a hat, in almost any light situation. The fundamental problem has not changed: there always being someone prepared to photograph an event on the QT. It would seem to be a common trait in the UK, and I have to admit, that I have often thought that I am in a trade with no professional registration requirements, unlike builders, electricians, etc., where there are controls, with safeguards for the customers, and income for the Tax Man.

Rugby & Badminton

I had moved my business from one location to another, including a short stay in a very small corner of a local old pub, The Llanover, and then an even smaller premises in Penuel Lane. Eventually I settled in to the basement of the building where I am now living and working. This period was also the outset of a new relationship, culminating in my second marriage, to Romela; followed shortly by the start of our new family, with Katy born in 1982 , and Richard in 1985.

At that time I was almost exclusively doing weddings and home child portraits, and opened quite short hours, giving me a chance to take part in some sporting activities. It was around then that I started to play badminton, at Abercynon and Hawthorn. At first I played casually with the Ynysybwl club, and occasionally with the Abercynon BC, both playing socially only. Before long, the desire to play league was too much, and I joined NTB club that played in Ystrad Mynach. They played in their own league, and soon I found myself in another club as well, playing in the Pontypridd and Rhondda Badminton League with the Rebels badminton club. The latter association lasted some time, while the former league soon was no more. I then looked to the Cardiff league to give me the quality and quantity of games to satisfy my desire for competitive sport.

With hindsight, I realise that I was overly competitive, often being somewhat over zealous in my approach. I am sure that I was just beginning to see myself in a true light, and the change from 'I am right' to 'I respect all' was taking hold. We all see things from our own perspective, and it is difficult to admit that we may have more to learn when we are in middle age.

I began to see myself as one of these older people around me, that have already gone through these thought processes, and had learnt to appreciate the thoughts of others. Sport is one of those activities that harness the thought processes into a particular channel. You can choose a selfish attitude, or not. I chose the non-selfish approach, respecting always the desires and views of opponents, although it took some years to take full control of myself, and stop the feelings of being cheated. Later, it was cricket that eventually got rid of any residual desires to react, and throw the toys out of the pram.

The badminton went from strength to strength, and with just one County appearance, I saw the potential to be a part of the grass roots of the sport, by taking on coaching, and took a course enabling me to be in charge of a class in Abercynon and elsewhere. This became a passion of mine, and soon overflowed into the club I was playing league badminton in. I suggested that the introduction of a junior section would greatly enhance the future of the club, but the then members rejected the idea. Soon I left to organise a new club specifically to promote the younger generation.

And so the Abercynon Junior Badminton Club was born. I am pleased to say it still functions in much the same way as it did originally. When I was no longer able to cope with the everyday running of the club, Peter, Leighton and Kevin Egan steadfastly continued to give many locals a good grounding in this most social of games. I still try to attend and do a little coaching once in a while. It always pleases me to see generation after generation learning the skills.

When we first formed, we attracted several new and very promising players, and within a year, were prominent in the Pontypridd & District League. A challenge had been put to me when I left the Rebels that we could not live in their league. One year later we enjoyed a clean sweep in the league, winning the Men's Doubles title without losing a single match, and beating my old club 9-0 and 8-1. In fairness their captain did acknowledge the achievement, which was much appreciated by me. It was the exuberance of the youth that always made me humble. To this day, I still get a kick out of seeing another new talent progress to success. So Peter and Co, keep up the great work, and make sure there is someone to take it on when you have to stop.

During my badminton era, I got involved in tournaments, and the running of same. When one of my men's doubles partners was killed in a road accident, a tournament was started in his memory. Denis was a vibrant 27 year old, in the prime of his life, when tragedy struck, and the successful tournament ran for many years, with an emphasis on fairness, based on an idea of mine that would channel players into their own ability sections, and then have three separate cups to play for. It proved successful, although, sadly, it does not seem to have been used anywhere that I know of since.

While the years of badminton had gone on, I encountered much trauma in my private life, the detail of which is irrelevant to the overall picture, but not to the effect it had on me personally. The struggle to see our two lovely children after the divorce proved to be most testing for everyone. So many made so many mistakes around that issue, that it is difficult to see how it could have happened. The hurt I felt left me, and everyone else involved, dazed and bewildered. It was to be four long years before I could see our two children again. But I can say that the one thing I learned in those years was patience and acceptance. I have no bad feelings at all with regard to that time, and although I will never understand how or why, I can say that the lesson learnt has made me stronger, as well as understanding 'Self' more clearly.

If I learned one specific lesson in all the anger and mistrust that ensued, it was that patience and a constant non-aggressive approach will bear fruit eventually. It is one of the most prominent memories that I have, when I received a phone call after all that time, saying, "dad, we want to see you". We have all never looked back since, and we all get on well, if not better than before.

During this upheaval, my dear mum died. She had been so ill for so long, especially after the tragedy with Bill had left her grieving in a way that is difficult to comprehend. And when she was admitted to hospital in late 1976, the doctors told me they were walking a mine-field, trying to treat so many problems at the same time. I could see her will ebbing away, and when I visited one evening, she whispered as I left, "I can't fight any longer". I cried all the way home, riding my scooter, and tried not to believe the inevitable, but early morning brought the news we never want to hear. She passed suddenly the next morning, and like all wonderful mums, will never be forgotten.

It is the only time I ever saw a doctor weeping, after he had given me the most glowing remarks about mum. The week or so she spent in East Glamorgan Hospital had touched more people than I had thought. Is it not strange, that we cannot teach the young the lessons that life will usually teach automatically?

I had moved to the basement of 3, Ceridwen Terrace, which I chose to have the address of 1a, Zion Street, in order that it would be easier to find for my customers, and so it proved. I traded from here for around ten years in all, and some of the commercial jobs that came my way were a little bizarre to say the least. One such job entailed recording the alleged trip an accused thief had taken, at night, along an unlit path along the side of a mountain, for some three miles. It turned out that there was no path, and how anyone could have found his way in the dark, was a complete mystery to me, as even in full daylight I had to scramble over hedges, under barbed wire fences, and across streams to reach the destination.

At the end of the trip I was met by the employing solicitor, who incidentally refused to join me on the journey, I had to report a drug addict I had come across in the final leg of my marathon, half conscious in a ditch. He had assured me he was O.K., but it was obvious that he was not. I never heard any more about the incident, but often wonder how he progressed from that state.

One other job that haunts me, is when I was to get evidence of the site of an affray that took place at a pub in the Gurnos Estate in Merthyr. It appeared that some sort of rivalry between two factions had boiled over one night into a pitched battle. One or two people had been hospitalised, and the case was a battle in court between the police on the one side, against the alleged perpetrators on the other. I was to present evidence for the police case, and I turned up to the said pub around nine o'clock one evening. I had to photograph the layout of the outside of the area, to show where the alleged incident had taken place. I was using fast film and a tripod to achieve the required pictures, and had set up the tripod to take the first shot, when a voice whispered over my shoulder, "what and who are you taking pictures for". Turning and seeing the most formidable, pint holding individual, looking like an all-in wrestler, posing the question, I realised swiftly that a lie was in this instant, appropriate.

"For the defence" I retorted, and he very casually returned to his mates waiting in the doorway of the pub. They watched my every move, sipping away at their beverages, and I stayed no longer than I had to when I finished the shoot.

I did another job for a solicitor involved in a kidnapping and murder case. It was all to do with two rival gangs, some stolen goods, and a fatality. On this case, the police insisted on giving us a police escort, as there was bad feeling on the site. I cannot go into details, but it illustrates the kind of work that arises once in a while.

I feel here, that I should explain, that my profession is not the subject of this book, but is merely a contributory factor in the overall aim, which is to document the autobiographical facts, and the way they affected the changes in my Karma, and my perceptions of that Karma. I believe that each event influences the mind-set, and ultimately changes the way we behave towards others, and how we perceive ourselves. The full and honest exploration of 'Self', has produced major changes in my outlook, making me smile more, and produced a more positive outlook, blaming only myself for any event that touches my day. Too often we see the litigation society of the modern day, distorting perceptions and attitudes. This is not just a monetary thing, but an attitude thing, which I believe is harming society.

So far, no one experience has changed that selfish start, but so many seeds have now been sown, that their cumulative effect, is sooner or later going to have a significant influence on the psyche.

Rugby had become a mild passion, and I had made some good friends with this interest. I was the classic nine-stone weakling, but still wanted to taste the thrill of playing. I took to training, with a not too serious commitment, and also become a regular supporter of Pontypridd RFC. Generally, I preferred to run the line with the linesman, taking photographs, as standing on the bob bank seemed too remote for me. The happy hours spent after the games were memorable in that you were all together, players and supporters, home and away.

These years were the amateur days in rugby, and I felt comfortable in the atmosphere generated by the sport, with friendly banter a constant companion of the travelling supporter. Stars of the day were, and still are, friends, having taken several of their wedding photographs over the years; It would be pretentious to name drop, but here are the first names of some: Bob, Allan, Mike, Tom, Chris, Steve, Steve 2, Joe, Paul, and Terry Andrews the sponge-man and physio. This man could make a corpse laugh, and when I felt a bit like one, he would always ease the pain, and make me laugh. His problem with my non-muscular body, was finding a muscle to work on, and the few I had frequently gave me problems. It was generally the badminton that caused the injury, and his expertise in locating and easing the problem, was a fairly regular occurrence for me. One such visit sticks in my mind, and always makes me smile. It was the shoulder that needed releasing, and as he worked my shoulder with his thumbs manipulating the offending muscle, he related the story of the Faith Healer. In print it just does not work, but anyone who has heard it, will know it is an acquired taste in jokes, but at the time it raised a laugh with me. But it was to be much later that it took a real hold on my mind. It was around three o'clock the following morning that I was in a state of two thirds asleep, and one third awake, that the humour of the story struck home. I was as close to hysterical as one can be, and every time I attempt to relate the story, I can never deliver the punch line for laughing.

Both Terry Andrews and Steve Cannon deserve huge thanks from me personally, and, I am sure, many others have benefited from their expertise over the years. Looking back now, it is ironic that such a physical game would have the effect of making me even more passive in my outlook, but the more I trained, and eventually played, the more entrenched the passive feelings became. I here must admit to have always been a passive character, or is a coward a more appropriate description, except for one occasion, age eighteen, when leaving the YMCA arm in arm with the then girlfriend. We were confronted by two youths who were intent on mischief, or simply fancied the girl on my arm. They proceeded to break the linked arms, and push me away from my girl friend. Totally surprised by this action, I reacted by calmly taking off my jacket, placing it on the stairs behind me, and turned to the two boys announcing, " I have to advise you, that I am in the SAS and can not be responsible for any consequences of any confrontation", and then stared at them calmly. The result has always amazed me, they turned and ran through the doorway and away along Taff Street. I could not have fought my way out of a paper bag, let alone handled two boys in a street fight, but it had been an instinctive reaction that had worked on that occasion.

I digress, back to the rugby experience, and the impending initiation into the pain of my first game for the Ponty Supporters side in Aberdare. We trained at Taff Vale Park in Treforest, but looking back, it was more like a picnic, and an excuse for not taking the wives shopping. The enthusiasm was immense, and as the great Sunday approached we were ready to take on the world. Unfortunately, we had to take on a pub side from Aberdare, that included some regular players ready to show us how it was really done. Naïve, spirited, enthusiastic and stupid would be a start in describing the game, but the enjoyment outstripped the pain and humiliation, and it was to be the start of many encounters over the next years.

In that particular game, we had a very fast full back called Wayne Hughes known as Skinny. He took the ball in midfield and started to run; unfortunately in the wrong direction, much to the amusement of all, especially the opposition. He eventually got the message to try the other direction, the end product of the run is now unknown, as we were too busy laughing to notice.

My prowess as a rugby player is legendary, as I know of no other that was as thin as me, or as bad as me, and I joke not. Strangely, I did enjoy the times playing, even when being flattened in the mud, especially one incident in Cardiff, when I, as the winger of all wingers, received a hospital pass from a certain flanker who will remain nameless. As I caught the ball, a twenty stone lump of jelly, (a prop forward) collided with me, he fell on top of me, making me feel like the fruit in a bowl of trifle, as the custard and cream is dumped on top. We landed in a mud bath, and as both could not move for exhaustion or hysterics, the game continued briefly as the ball had gone back to our backs. I have only a recollection of being half covered in mud, after the jelly had been levered away from me. A photo of me after this incident still sits on a sideboard, to remind me of this encounters.

In the four or five years that I attempted to play the game, I managed just one try in a six-a-side game at Ynysangharad Park in Pontypridd. Not that that in itself is as important as the new friends made, with Larry, Islwyn, Terry, Paul and many more, still rated as good friends.

The short adventure came to an end soon after a game with Morganstown RFC, when I tackled a rather heavy opponent, who landed on my knee sideways, damaging some ligaments, and causing a week of considerable discomfort. It affected my business, and I came to the conclusion that a less physical sport would be more appropriate at my age.

A new relationship dawned, filling a void that we all need, and it was to prove a strong influence, eventually producing two more great offspring. The only very slight regret is that none of the offspring seem to want to have any part in the business I have built up. Donald is the most likely to date, becoming a very fine camera repair expert, until manufacturers stopped supplying spare parts.

Slowly but surely, I was becoming more content, with the move to our new home at Vale Gardens, giving some great family years of comparative normality. Badminton was the only sport for now, and although finances were not particularly good, the introduction of One Hour Processing of colour films was to set a new direction to my business. I was approached by a local business consortium, to run the processing machine at their shop in Pontypridd, and could continue my professional trading at the same time. Romela and Donald worked along side me, and overall it was successful. We were situated on Taff Street, which was the main shopping area, and the only drawback that eventually became apparent, was the fact that we were on a corner.

This seemed to have quite an effect on business, and with hindsight, people were conscious of the dangerous road situation, and did not notice the shop as perhaps they should. Space was a problem, and soon it became more of a problem, when the owners of the processing machine wanted out. I was offered the machine, and eventually bought the whole deal, running the combined business under my own name.

All went well until a massive rise in rent, meant the business would not be feasible at that location, and the option was to find an alternative location. Problems with the length of the lease to go, meant a severe burden on our finances, and it was to take years, and much effort to resolve the problem.

I had noticed that the building where I had spent many years working from the basement, was up for rent. I thought it would be worth inquiring into the possibility of buying. This proved to be the best business move of my life, so far. The property was owned by Mrs. Macbean, the mother of John, a school buddy from the Grammar School days. He had been a very successful chiropodist, and now resided in Carmarthen, on a farm with his family, including his mum. We had not met for some years, and it was a great reunion when I turned up at his farm to discuss the property. After some reminiscing, we discussed the possibility of purchase, as opposed to renting the property, and Mrs Macbean said that as it was an old friend, she would agree.

We duly completed the necessary paper work, and set about the transfer of all the equipment from the old shop. Much had to be done, and it was a long and backbreaking move, considering the complexity of the machine. Donald was a rock at that juncture, with his amazing abilities to repair and fix almost anything, he got the machine running in no time.

The property had been divided into three separate areas in order for lettings to be offered, with the basement having been a store room, along with an outside toilet, and an area adjoining the back door the size of a kitchen, but open to the elements on the one side. This had in a previous occupation, been used as a milk storage area for the then occupants, who ran a milk delivery business.

The outside toilet was now obsolete, and so the first job was to remove it, and at the same time, make an entrance for a car-port, removing the high part of the wall and making good stonework, to comply with local council requirements. This done, we had to start making a living, and try to get rid of the debt and the overdraft. The money left by dear mum had helped to pay much of the house costs, and I was determined not to repeat the dilemma of the previous money emergency.

The ground floor had two rooms, the front shop area, and the back room for the processing and finishing, while the first floor was available to rent out. This we did, and it played a big part in keeping us on track financially, with a hairdresser, Tattoo Studio and a mediation company at different times in occupation.

It must be said here, that one of my failings I had not yet got under control, was my rare, but frightening temper. I had never understood, or even tried to fathom, what was the trigger for these outbursts of frustration, and the scars of some of these explosions, I still carry today. I seem to remember that it was as though I was driving towards a cliff face, with no means of stopping, eventually colliding with myself. If I were carrying a box or mug, it would be released in a major release of energy, resulting in breakages, and often a very sore fist or foot that had collided with a hard object. I never released the frustration on any person, but I realise that it must have been unnerving for the onlooker.

I had developed a strategy of dissipating this energy, by leaving the situation immediately, and giving time for the feelings to subside, but I am sure that these actions were not understood by those in close proximity, and to any recipients of these actions, I give here a full and unreserved apology. I feel no desire to blame anyone but myself, as it is the self that acts or reacts to situations, and this is now fundamental to my attitude to life.

I have recognised some of the reasons for my actions, and it is noticeable that the occurrences are now gone, although I am more aware if a situation is on the horizon, and have the ability to snuff it out before it takes hold.

Badminton was in full swing now, and both Romela and myself were keen players in the local leagues. I became an intermediate coach myself, and teaching in several venues around our area. Most of all was the involvement with the club I had formed in Abercynon. Over the years, generations of youngsters have gained some knowledge of the game. I trust this will continue, giving them the ability to partake in a team sport that offers a healthy option to many traits that seem to be familiar in some other sports.

Romela played until very close to her delivery of our first, Katy, but at least I was at hand on this occasion, not so with Richard. I had organised a tournament on 13th. July, and Romela had been admitted to East Glamorgan Hospital the day before. I had phoned to check on progress on the ward, and on the inquiry at around two o'clock, when the tournament was in full swing, I was reliably informed by the nurse that there was a long way to go, and to ring again in two hours.

Richard arrived a short time later, and I did not get a message for some time. When I eventually got to the Hospital, I was presented to the new arrival, who was overdue by the way, to state, along with Romela, that he looked like ET and was temporarily called Wally.

Here, I must explain that within two days he was transformed into a prize specimen, and I hope he can forgive me for these ramblings.

One or two highlights of the badminton era are worthy of a mention. The earliest I recall was at Ystrad Mynach Sports Centre playing for the NTB badminton club, in the final game of the season, on which hinged the winning or losing of the league title. There are three pairs of men in each team, with each pair playing each other, giving a total of nine games to decide the match. A win by five matches to four would be enough for either team to win. My regular partner could not play that night, so one of the second team stepped up to partner me as the third pair, winning our opening match against their third pair.

That really was our job done, although losing to the second pair, it was up to our top pairs to see us home. Unfortunately, they only managed to win three out of six, meaning the last game between us, and the top opposition, to decide the match. They had not lost that night, with the outlook rather bleak, especially when they took the first of three rubbers. At this point our team-mates left for a shower, with a resignation to the inevitable.

My partner and I made it to the changing room, to be faced by some very gloomy faces, tentatively asking the score, which we gave them, just with the points tally without saying who had scored which, but when the even more gloomy opposition arrived, they immediately realised we had pulled off the impossible, and won. The pleasure of that night's entertainment will long be remembered, with both Dave and I the toast of our club. It is so pleasing that sport throws up these unexpected results from time to time, provided the participants can respect both sides of the coin.

To Tom Gunning, Garry and the rest of the boys who celebrated with us that night, thanks for another great experience, with one more "To The League", the phrase used over and over that night, in the race for a reasonable intoxication. This win shows one side of the coin; the next illustrates the other, hopefully demonstrating the dignity required in both instances.

The game was for the Lek-Tech team in Cardiff, run by Tony Backhouse, this being a mixed-doubles match against a young Beddau side. On this occasion, I was partnered by my wife, Romela; and yet again, the result depended on this match. It was the best of three games, the score being one game all, going in to the decider. The final game was a one-way procession, getting to match point in our favour, with just one point for victory. Not even with eight match points could we see the end, in our favour, and the very young couple from Beddau took the honours, and deservedly so.

There must be a significance to my clear recollection of that night, as I remember the admiration I had for the couple who had achieved, what had seemed unachievable. This was the other side of the coin, it being the earliest incident, where I felt more admiration for my opponents, than disappointment for myself, and my partner.

In another incident, I was playing a men's doubles, this time in Cardiff, again with a stand-in partner, Allan Green. He was a good friend off court, but this was his first call-up to the first team. He was the most enthusiastic of players, always giving his all, and never giving up. The situation was very similar to the previously described men's doubles, but with a different club. We were the last game on again, and again the league title depended on the outcome. It was very late in the evening, the centre staff allowing us to go overtime, in order to complete the match. The result was supposed to be a formality to our opponents, and when they got to match point, it was all nearly over.

After several match points we battled back to take the second game, squaring the match at one game all. By this time, all our club mates had seen a possible upset on the cards, along with a few staff, eager to see the conclusion. Everything again was on the last game, and I have to admit to being somewhat tired, so I asked for the regulatory ten minute break to recover, proceeding to meditate, lying on the courtside to recharge the batteries. I distinctly felt positive vibes, when Allan and I took to the court for the final game. We had a total belief in our game plan, and proceeded to sweep to a convincing victory over our opponents, who earlier had been supremely confident of an easy win.

We did not see the side we had beaten to the league title, until the following season, when we were shocked to hear that the two players in that final game had not played since. I found that very sad, if, in fact it was true, hoping they learnt some of the lessons I had taken on board, making the experience of winning and losing, equally enjoyable.

Back in Abercynon Juniors, another incident of a different nature pleased me no end. It was a tournament, and I was playing a mixed-doubles game against one of my long-time students. Tim Mapp had started as a youngster many years earlier, always striving to beat his teacher. This was to be his day, giving him obvious pleasure. It also gave me the great satisfaction, of seeing him come of age on court. We shook hands, with me realising, that would probably be the last time I would match his ability on court. So it proved to be.

I realise now that these incidents were having a significant influence on my attitudes to life in general. The best way I can describe this, is that it is rather like viewing life through a camera lens in the telephoto position, and as I zoom back to wide-angle, the whole picture becomes more and more complete. The changes were imperceptible while the moment was there, yet it all seems so clear looking back.

A pleasant interlude around this period was a trip to Berlin with Pontypridd Rugby Football Club. Tom David led the troops on an unforgettable expedition, playing three games against mostly military sides, but generally, we were there to take in the wonders of that magical city. I was particularly keen to see how much it had changed since my last visit. We were billeted in Spandau Barracks, next door to the prison where Rudolf Hess was in residence. I can still see the old man walking with guards, in the grounds of the prison, albeit from a good distance away.

Here I must explain that I had never been a drinker of alcohol, but got caught up in the typical rugby tour norm of the occasional tipple. It only took a little to make me tipsy, and I became very much the worse for wear, after a session in the NAAFI. The next day we were due to visit East Berlin in a coach, via Checkpoint Charlie, and I was unable to join the boys. There is always a silver lining, and a day or two later, one of the older members wanted to make a visit to a cemetery for allied airmen, and then see Checkpoint Charlie.

This proved to be traumatic, as when we arrived at the cemetery, I simply could not enter the gates, something literally stopped me from moving forward through the magnificent entrance. I become overwhelmed by the sight of the thousands of gravestones, immaculately kept, geometrically aligned, and sweeping, it seemed, to infinity. It was too much for me, so I waited while my friend, a former airman, paid his respects to his fallen comrades. This had been another occasion when I had become emotional in a situation that seemingly had no relevance to me, or my past.

Our minds turned to our next port of call, Checkpoint Charlie. This occasion reversed the mindset, and it was my turn to be in an old haunt, and my companion to be the first time visitor. After a short visit to the East, which was uneventful, we returned to visit the Museum very close to the Checkpoint, in the West. All the old methods used to escape from the East were still there from my earlier visit, and it really is an eye opener to any visitor who is interested in the history of that period. On leaving the Museum, I suggested we should get a souvenir of the visit, and gouge a piece of the wall to take home. My friend thought that a little radical, and pointed out the East German guards overlooking the scene. He withdrew to a safe distance, and tentatively watched as I walked straight up to the wall, and prised a large piece, enough for the two of us. I saw no danger, and there was none, so perhaps we had started the process of getting rid of the wall.

There is a tradition on such tours, of a medallion passed from one member of the party to another; ours was 'Spewer of the Week', and the incumbent had to witness another of the party, in such endeavour, and could then pass it on to that person. I duly obliged the previous owner after a visit to a Beer Garden, where I had fallen foul of the dreaded alcohol. I subsequently wore the medallion around my neck for three weeks, not able to pass it on until a week after our return to Wales.

Although I was the official photographer for the trip, that really was only in name, as it was just an excuse for being there. I did photograph the regular groups, and captured one or two interesting incidents. One such occasion was the visit of all of the party to the Stadium Olympic, where a certain leader held some famous rallies in the darker days of history, followed by a certain member of our party mimicking one of those infamous appearances from the very point that he had stood, all those years before. The rugby that day was played on a ground there in the stadium, with a later return to the centre of Berlin for a short tour. It was here that one of the party called 'Spiders'. To explain, this was another silly habit on such tours, where each member of the tour, can call just once, "Spiders". On hearing this call, everyone in the group has to lay on their backs, and wave their arms and legs in the air, like an overturned arachnid.

We were on the main shopping area of Berlin when this call came; the reaction of the rather reserved German shoppers was to be expected, with some of the descriptions of us, quite easy to interpret. I did get a shot of this silly spectacle, after spidering for a reasonable time with the thirty or so grown men performing well on a wide pavement, right in the centre of the town.

Some of the stars of this tour included our captain, along with his fellow back row Mike Shellard and Chris Seldon, both of whom had served in the Welsh Guards in that great city. Returning on the plane, I recall an exceptional round of applause when we eventually made a safe landing, indicating to me, that a number of the squad were more than a little nervous of flying. Overall, it was a most memorable trip with a group of great guys, including a legend in Pontypridd RFC, Mr Terry Andrews the physio and master joke man. He is one of the most positive men I have ever met, and seems to be able to smile whenever it is needed. I must here mention a gentleman of these, and many other days, Bob Pemberthy, the gentle giant, respected for his ability on the field of play, and his steadfast loyalty, appreciated by one and all.

I deem it a privilege to have been associated with the club, especially at a period when sport was still sport, where respect was normal between opponents and team-mates, and there was a sharing culture that gave a feeling of well being. Although I have moved on to new challenges, I keep those years as special in my memory, along with all the photographs I took of the great visiting, and home teams, still on show on the walls of the club.

My personal highlight of those years, was a cartoon in the *Western Mail* by Gren in his Ponty and Pop strip, when he described a certain valley club, (he left it to the reader), where the photographer was faster than some of the wingers. I choose to think I may have prompted the quote in some way.

My days as a rugby player drew swiftly to a halt, playing the last few games for the supporters side as Super-Sub. All this meant, was that I could stroll around the touchline for an hour, then give some tired player an early shower. In most cases, I never touched the ball in those ten minutes or so. All in all, they were enjoyable days, although I am sure some of the injuries are still with me today. Also with me, a group of friends second to none, with their influences far outweighing the negatives.

These years were the usual struggle to make ends meet, always checking the overdraft, but rapidly dropping materialism, and taking on a more philosophical attitude, with, "C'est la vie" becoming more the attitude, going with the flow, accepting the end product of each day. Along with this attitude, was a desire to remove the stresses of everyday life, by being more positive, thinking more and more along the lines of Buddhist teachings, although here I must admit it was more a desire than a fact.

An image that haunted me regularly, was that of a Buddhist Monk demonstrating his total control of self, and taking his own life, making a statement about an issue that he felt strongly about. He was prepared to give his life for the cause, demonstrating a self-control beyond anything I can imagine, but a mindset that humbles me. He accepted death, with the pain in achieving that end not apparent, showing no sign of anguish, only a peaceful demeanour, with total dignity. In life, there are events and images that seem to ring bells in your soul. This was one of those, slowly but surely moulding the next years of the existence. The everyday toils, along with the constant joy of facing new challenges, meeting new peoples, and encountering different cultures, were the distractions that made every day a challenge and a revelation. It was now that the situation would throw me in a new direction.

Sport had been an integral part of our lives, the whole family sharing in activities, although there were the beginnings of tensions in our marriage, unfortunately not fully recognised by me at the time. Some holidays gave some respite from the work toils, with one or two holidays being memorable for the wrong reasons. One visit to Corfu had all the hallmarks of a perfect antidote to the rigours of the workplace, and so it started, my eldest daughter joining us for the first time on a holiday.

The five of us settled in to a small friendly hotel, with their own small pool, and basic but adequate facilities. The only one who could not make it was Donald, but with Romela, Richard, Katy, Helga and myself, we were ready for the sunshine, along with the sounds and sights of this lovely island.

There was a lively set of people in our hotel, and their exuberance in and around the pool was usually evident, always giving one confidence of having someone around in an emergency. There were no lifeguards around the pool, which was the norm in these resorts, resulting in a near disaster on one warm, quiet afternoon. There were few in the pool that afternoon, with Katy, Rom and myself, relaxing on the sun-bed. I watched as Richard and Helga enjoyed the cool of the pool, although both were not strong swimmers, they enjoyed messing about in the water. As this was the first time on holiday together, neither was aware of the others strengths in the swimming department. Helga was gently swimming the length of the pool towards the deep end, while Richard was swimming towards her. As their paths collided, Richard clung to Helga's neck, hoping for security to gather his breath. The result was immediate, both sank like stones, luckily with me watching,

With one deep breath, I left the sun-bed, and dived in, I must here admit to being a poor swimmer, with the only saving grace, an ability to swim under water better than on the surface. When I got to them they were clinging to each other, so I grabbed Richard, pulled him to one side, and returned him to the surface, pushing him to the side of the pool. I immediately dived back to Helga who was struggling to regain her composure, and used the same technique on her, returning her to safety. After the event we realised how easily situations can arise, sometimes with dire consequences, however not on this occasion.

Another experience on this holiday was to be a day out with just

Romela and myself. We had decided to take a boat trip to Albania, which had only recently attained a new beginning politically, and had opened its doors to visitors for the first time in years. As we approached the small port, many children swam around the boat indicating they would dive for any money thrown in, so dangerous we thought, but as the day progressed, so did the understanding of the situation.

Going ashore, it became very obvious that the poverty was extreme, but the welcome was warm and friendly, so while the main party from the boat went off to a local bar for home-made lemonade, I decided to explore a little. I wandered the couple of roads where there were a few shops, and was amazed to find they were all bare of any goods, except the shoe shop that had just a few pairs on display. I remember the bread shop was empty with a sign giving times of the next availability of stock. The only people were the children waiting around the dock area, all well behaved and polite, waiting, as we found out later, for the tourists to return to the boat.

I wandered further, to savour the atmosphere, and came across a group of men unloading a large truck of melons. Not knowing the language at all, I indicated a greeting, stopping to watch a while, quickly to be surrounded by inquisitive youngsters, along with the men unloading the melons. They really tried to make me accept a gift of one of the melons, but it was quite impractical for me to carry such an item, and I had to try to be respectful of their generosity, without offending them. It would seem that although they had very little, they were prepared to share with a total stranger, the little they had, this being a common occurrence in many of the poorer nations that I have had the privilege of witnessing. In particular, it struck me as similar to the meetings with the people of Iran many years earlier.

It was late afternoon when the party returned to the boat, and as we gathered on the quay, many of the local children and teenagers gathered to see what could be gleaned from the visitors, whether diving for money, or just mixing with the affluent visitors. They admired tee-shirts worn by some of us, with many of us parting with items and money to the well mannered kids, one of whom seemed a little meek amongst his peers. He and a couple of others had seen me as a soft touch, and had clearly indicated a liking for my watch, and I decided that he should get the said watch. I worked out a strategy to give him a good chance of retaining the watch, as it was clear that some of the older boys could easily bully it off him if they got a chance.

I gave almost all the few possessions I had with me, and then said that was it, but eventually getting the watch surreptitiously to the small boy, without the others noticing. The reaction was wonderful, his eyes said it all, our smiles rebounded back and forth for a moment or two, then he turned, and ran like the wind along the quay, glancing back just once that I noticed, and disappeared around a corner, to show his gift to his family or friends. Such a small gesture had such reactions, that it reinforced many mindsets that had been brewing in my mind for years.

I had little sympathy on the return journey, when I was very cold, wearing only my shorts, but on reflection, I would do the same again for selfish reasons, as the pleasure it gave me, makes me want more of those same feelings. I do occasionally wonder if the young lad used the timepiece to good advantage, and that he has progressed in his journey through life so far successfully, and has fulfilled his dreams.

An earlier holiday provided an experience of a slightly different nature, a visit to Malta turned out to be somewhat painful. It all started so well on this friendly island, with warm weather and good company, as well as the pleasures of the Fiestas, which were in full swing. A slight pain in the shoulder gradually got worse, spreading to the back and arm. It was a pain that did not fit the normal muscular sprains, and after twenty-four hours, was so bad we called a doctor. After an injection, the pain grew even stronger, and I must admit to being a little worried.

Finally, an ambulance was called by the hotel to take me to the hospital in Valletta, a distance of some twelve miles. The vehicle was very small, and the driver a retired rally man, or something similar, as he took great delight in driving at top speed along rather uneven roads, causing considerable discomfort to his passengers. He had obviously taken possession of this vehicle with a new siren and flashing lights, taking full advantage of these, he proceeded the whole way in full voice. I cannot say that it was the best journey of my life so far, but it was one of the most memorable.

I was placed on a ward, along with some lovely locals who were all so supportive of this youngish foreigner in some distress. I must have disturbed many that first night, as the pain seemed to intensify, much to the doctors puzzlement. Try as they did, there was little change for those first days.

Here, let me describe the wonderful hospital as I saw it. The building was a stereotype of the forties or fifties, very much like the Cottage Hospital on the Common in Pontypridd. The wards were the most basic, yet I felt completely safe, with the staff showing a dedication that shone through the conditions they worked with. There was one elderly gent in the next bed to myself, suffering with a serious leg problem, and I clearly recall no sign of distress, but a calm acceptance of whatever the future held for him. Uncomplaining, cheerful, with always a smile, especially when his wife visited, returning an even bigger smile.

Neither spoke very much English, but the few words we exchanged showed me they were charming and caring people, making me feel very much at home in their country. One evening, after two or three days of injections and treatment, that had given no respite, and shortly after the end of a visit from my family, I became aware of a lifting of the pain in a sudden reversal of the past few days, resulting in a remarkable recovery.

I was kept in for another day, to be sure I was making a full recovery, allowing me to return to my holiday with my wife after her next visit. The doctors admitted they were puzzled as to what had caused the pain, but admitted they suspected a heart attack at first, but concluded some kind of muscle spasm was the cause. They told me they could not understand the reason for the recovery, but as they said, the body can sort itself out in some circumstances, and this was one of those occasions.

Just before my release, as I awaited the arrival of my family, the wife of the gent in the adjoining bed came to speak to me. In very broken English she gently asked if the pain had subsided, continuing that she had been distressed by the obvious pain I had been in, and after her visit days earlier, she had gone to the Chapel at the Hospital to say a prayer. Later, when I perused the events, it became very clear, that it was the very same evening of my remarkable recovery.

I leave it to the individual to come to their own conclusions, but it reinforced my own conviction, that we all have massive powers of healing through will power, both for others, and ourselves. I shall never forget the kindness shown me by that couple, along with the care shown to a foreigner in their small country. We should all remember how small the world is, and how similar all the people of that world are.

These two occurrences highlight the impermanence of life to me, and make me acutely aware of the need to look in at ourselves, to assess, and then attain a peaceful existence. I am quite sure that these, along with other experiences, have pushed me to a greater understanding of myself, and subsequently, of others, reinforcing the quote from years before, of, "know yourself, and you will know others".

Bryan, myself and Bill, in 1940 and 1945

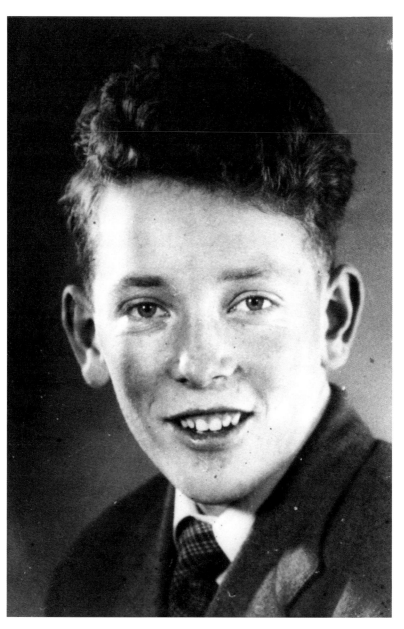

At my first job, Ivor Alderson Studio, 1956

THE SAVILLE PLAYERS
in
"NO ROOM AT THE INN"
By JOAN TEMPLE
CHARACTERS (in order of appearance):

Norma Smith .... Lesley Lloyd
Judith Drave .... Kathleen Cravos
Ronnie Chilbury .... Derek Lewis
Mary O'Rane .... Vivienne Carslake
Kate Grant .... Shirley Teague
Mr. Burrells .... Burgess Hunt
Inspector Willis .... David Mann
Mrs. Voray .... Olivia Irving
Mrs. Waters .... Sheila Ashdown
Terence O'Rane .... John O'Byrne
The Rev. James Allworth .... Tommy Leaver
The Play Produced and Stage Directed by
DAVID MANN
Stage Manager: SHEILA ASHDOWN
Settings by the Saville Players

Synopsis of Scenes
PROLOGUE
The living room of a small house in a "Safe Area"
one morning in January

ACT I
Scene 1—The Same (a late afternoon in the previous June.
Scene 2—The same (a Saturday night a fortnight later.

INTERVAL
(During Interval Light Refreshments will be served in the Theatre Cafe. Also a Licensed Bar for Patrons.

ACT II
Scene 1—Rev. James Allworth's study (ten days later).
Scene 2—The same as Act One (some weeks later).

ACT III
Scene 1—The same (one night in January).
Scene 2—The same (two hours later).

EPILOGUE
The living room (the following morning).

THE SAVILLE PLAYERS express their sincere thanks for the kind loan of furniture, etc., to Messrs. Bowns (Antiques), Tudor Williams, Astons, Brown Bros & Taylor, also Fred Fey, Esq., for piano and all musical effects.

Patrons are reminded that the Box Office is open after this performance and seats may be booked for NEXT WEEK when the SAVILLE PLAYERS present

"THE SACRED FLAME"
By W. SOMERSET MAUGHAM

Saturday, March 10, 1956   OBSERVER, LEAD

Members of the cast of "Give Me Your Hand."

YOUNG COMPANY TRIUMPHS IN 'STRONG MEAT' PLAY

IT is announced that the play, "Give me your hand," presented by the Pontypridd Boys' Club juniors has been adjudged the best of the eight plays performed during the recent Pontypridd and District Youth Drama Festival. The company has been awarded an 'A' certificate and will now compete in the county youth finals at Aberdare in April.

Treading the Boards, 1954 and 1956

First car – 'TIZA BUGA' – Isle of Sheppey, 1959

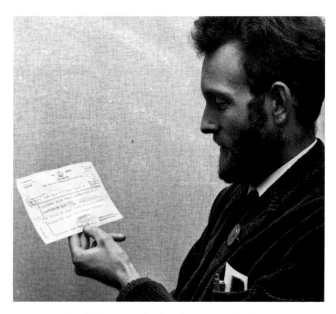

Royal Telegram – On Appointment as Chairman
of Welsh Young Liberals, 1965

First studio – Bridge Street, Pontypridd, 1967

Barry Butlins Photographers, 1970

Athens, 1973

Brecon, 1976

'Spiders' – Pontypridd R.F.C in Olympic Stadium, Berlin, 1981

Pontypridd Rugby Supporters Club, at Rhymney, 1982

Gas bottle explosions at Old Bridge, Pontypridd, 7 May 1985

Abercynon Juniors Badminton Club, 1988

In action, 1988

Pontypridd C.C. 3rd XI, 1995

Creigiau 2nd XI vs Llantwit Major, 1999

Kathmandu Temple, 2002

Kathmandu, 2002

Kathmandu – Boys living in makeshift tent next to University cricket ground, 2002

65th Birthday with Wonderbrass, 2005

Outside my studio, 2005

Qutb Minar, Delhi

Taj Mahal, 2006

Sameep & Neeru with Jonathan and myself, Delhi, 2006

Jazz & Teaching

At the same juncture in my career, I undertook a job at Coed-y-lan Comprehensive School as an extra-curricular tutor in photography, taking any interested students to a modest level through the City and Guilds scheme. The privilege of imparting knowledge to these eager beavers was a diversion that had not occurred to me before, and was to prove both motivating and satisfying.

It all began solely as an interest for the students, with no certificate at the end of it, but quickly progressed to the City and Guilds diploma, adding some points to their tally for their entry to a University. At first I was given students in their final year of 'A' Level, all of whom were eager to learn, making the task most pleasurable. My interaction with the teaching staff was another big plus, giving me an insight into the stresses, pressures, pleasures, along with a host of other descriptions of the noble art of Teaching.

The skills I witnessed in so many of these often unsung heroes, changed my perception of a profession that seems to have been much devalued over the years, yet amongst the students themselves, you will always find a strong regard for their tutors, admitting often that their influences were key to their successes. For me to have touched the edges of this culture was a privilege.

I shall not embarrass any one of these now adult workers, but they have become friends, often working in and around the photographic industry, but in all cases, they remain a welcome addition to a galaxy of people I am honoured to have as friends. I shall give the first names of some of the students, in no order in particular. Martin, Sally-Ann, Paul, John, Ceri, Joanne, Angharad, along with a host of names that elude this ageing memory of mine. One amusing post-script on one of these was imparted to me some years after at the wedding of one of my students. Her father told the guests that she had returned from school one evening to inform her parents that she was going to become a physiotherapist. Well Ceri, you made it!

Two students stand out in my memory for perhaps the wrong reasons, although unknown to them, they taught me a lesson. They were two students who really did not want to be there at all, consequently giving rise to some difficult and challenging situations. Their youthful zest for fast action, created a tricky situation within a class of some less zestful individuals. As my subject is very much a hands-on subject, I found a way of dissipating their energies by making them the racing participants, in an exercise to get photos of fast moving objects. They were the targets of the other students camera work, while they showed to their mates how fast they were on the running track. After two or three re-takes, they were suitably tired, leaving the remainder of the lesson, a more peaceful place for one and all.

I recall feeling there was no hope for these individuals at that time, yet to my great satisfaction, they showed in the years after leaving the school, considerable abilities in their work ethic, but most of all, were always amongst the most respectful of individuals when we met.

These events reinforced my faith in the individual, as well as the impermanence of a norm, for it is only our perception of the norm, that makes it such in our own mind. The nine years spent imparting the knowledge I had acquired to these students, were amongst the most satisfying of my photographic career, pushing me further towards a peaceful co-existence with 'Self'.

It was to be a new beginning in the early 90s, with back pains limiting my ability to play badminton, resulting in more and more coaching, rather than playing. An old friend suggested I bring my old trombone to a rehearsal for a forthcoming play, with me expecting it to be used by some member of the cast. Oh no, he wanted me to play, not realising that I could not. It took a great deal of persuading for me to agree to take part in this experimental production. I had sworn to myself many years before, never to take any part in a play again. I was assured that it would only involve making the odd noise on the trombone, and so it turned out.

Valley of the Kings was the play written by Laurence Allan, one of my fellow rugby stars from our Supporters side of a few years earlier. His enthusiasm, along with the musical director, Paula Gardner, got me a seat in the small ensemble of real musicians, savouring the delights of making music, or in my case, noises. I am assured that I was noticed at one of the rehearsals, not for my total lack of musical skill, but for my ability to allow the trombone slide to come adrift from the main body of the instrument, leaving me somewhat bemused, and the observers amused.

I remember very little of the production itself, except I was invited to attend a community jazz band, where I could hone my musical skills and simply join in the music making, without any pressures or demands, joining in at the rear of the stages when they played the occasional gig, getting a feel for the buzz that such activity can generate. Rob Smith and Jess ran the weekly practice sessions, with Denise Lord the organiser. This was to become fifteen years of fun and learning, meeting a whole new group of great people, all intent on expressing themselves in their own way.

Wonderbrass was the name of this great group of people that I had been drawn to, and while I made no pretence of being a musician then, or since, I derived huge enjoyment from playing the few notes I could manage, and being a part of a group of people intent on making their own brand of music. The patience of Rob was an inspiration, for he never showed any reaction when we played something really badly, and treated everyone with the same respect.

The band of some thirty players, would fill many a stage with their energy; spurring the audiences into dancing, clapping and general excitement, not so much for their great musicianship, but for their exuberance and endeavour. The leader Rob held everything together, with his considerable talent, both as a musician and a leader. Behind us all was Mark O'Conner on drums, giving the whole band a solid base to work over.

The band travelled to many towns and cities at home and abroad. One of the most memorable was to the Cork Jazz Festival, where we stayed for several days, playing a couple of gigs, one in a hotel. There were three floors being used, and the crowds would wander from one venue to the next, as bands came and went throughout the day. We set up for our slot, without many people in attendance, but no sooner had we started on the first tune, 'Scaravan', than people appeared from everywhere, filling the hall in no time.

Our line up on that occasion was smaller than in later years, but the regulars that I recall from then, were Eros Sax, Howard Sax, Richard Trumpet, Nick Trombone and Lloyd George Electric Bass. My apologies to those not mentioned, but the gig was particularly poignant for me, it being the first time I felt a real part of the band, playing the odd lick with a confidence not previously present.

Strangely, it remains clearly one of the best received gigs I can recall, with the Irish audience exceedingly vocal in their appreciation of our efforts. Brecon Jazz would also be a focal point to work towards each year, that August slot the one date everyone looked forward to, working that little bit harder to ensure the best possible results.

Practice night was every Tuesday, the venue The Hollybush in Hopkinstown, where the back room would resound to a torrent of sound from this Community Band, comprising a cross section of players of all abilities. Our numbers would always be changing, with some joining while others moved on, and it was the unique nature of the band that made it so special to so many of us. There were the young, up and coming players, looking for a vehicle to hone their skills, finding a direction for their particular talents, and there were many who just wanted to experiment and derive some enjoyment out of making music.

Most new members would begin nervously, holding back from trying a solo, sometimes, as in my case, for years. Eventually we all succumbed to the lure of playing up front, and it would always be rewarded with a whoop and a holler from the band, giving you the confidence to move on. It mattered, not a jot how good or bad the playing was, the reaction was always positive, giving one a sense of achievement, which, of course, it was.

A London trip springs to mind, when a bus turned up to transport us to the venue showing serious signs of wear and tear. As my son Richard was also playing in this particular gig, I decided to collect my car and drive to London. A wise decision as it turned out, as the bus duly broke down half way. We played in a pub in south London, near the Elephant and Castle, and if I am not mistaken, it was the first meeting with Jim Barrett (Double Bass) who was living in London at the time. Jim has become a good friend since moving back to Wales, and now plays the magnificent Bass Saxophone in the band.

Our son Richard played the Alto Sax, and being only twelve was a little nervous. However Gaynor, a fellow Alto player, took him under her wing, giving him much support and guidance. As we prepared to leave the gig, a lady asked Richard for his autograph, lavishing praise on him, and fully expecting him to become the next great star of the jazz world, so pick up that Sax again Rich.

Richard only stayed a while with the band, but I am sure he could re-kindle the desire at a later date. Around then, we had our first visit to the Druidstone Hotel in Pembroke. It was to become an iconic venue for several visits, with its vista over the Irish sea, a sight to fill a large section of anyone's memory bank. The evenings would be spent jamming in the downstairs bar, until the early hours, with uninhibited performances by one and all. Andy Roberts (Sop Sax), one of a succession to delight and amuse, Lauren, Sarah, Patrick, Anthony and Pol on Altos, all crammed into the small space available.

Jane, our host, put up with our late nights with a permanent smile, showing an obvious liking for the spontaneous nature of our music, and the food provided was more than adequate for us hungry souls. The mornings after were a little slow getting going, but as a non-drinker myself, I was usually one of the first to surface, getting the early view of the magnificent scenery, with the chance of an early walk onto the headland. One must for me personally, was to sit in a shelter there, and meditate a while, watching the waves roll in from the Irish Sea. A plaque on the wall made the spot particularly poignant, as it was placed by relatives of a young lad who, "So Loved That Spot" during his short life. If any reader wants a peaceful day out, go spend an hour there, and rest your soul.

The weekend usually ended with a celebratory gig, entertaining the diners at Sunday lunch. Crammed into the first floor dining room, we would play in small groups, alternating players between numbers, much to the obvious delight of the diners. Dominant players in each section were, Brett (Flute) Jenny (Baritone Sax) Pete and Rich. (Trombones), with one of the visits including Steff. Richard (Trumpet) was joined by the ever lively Mike on at least one occasion, raising a smile and his ever present hat to amuse the audience.

It became a tradition at some point in the weekend, to arrange a game of beach rugby, with the tide sequence having been researched well in advance. Little can be said about such events, other than the bruises were often prominent for a few days, but it did clear the lungs for the next rehearsal. In later visits, beach cricket took equal position in the weekend's events, with a certain Simon (Drums) stealing the limelight, with some impressive hitting. Some of the more hardy souls took to the ocean for some chilly swims, even though it was often late in the season for such activities. Denise, Fiona and Manon were the regulars.

The bonding of these events, along with the regular gigs we were doing, formed long and strong friendships amongst the diverse characters in the group. People like Joanne (Double Bass), Bedwr (Sax), Fiona (percussion), Nick Briggs (Sax), Jackie (Double Bass), Howard (Alto), not to mention Stewart-the-laugh (Tenor Sax). So many more it makes my brain hurt, but all, and I do mean all, were greatly appreciated by myself, their charismatic collective leaves me with a glow in my memory that will not diminish.

I would like here to pay tribute to two people in particular; Richard (Trumpet) who put up with my visits to Stow Hill for advice and such, and Denise, who must have put so much time and effort into making the band so successful, that I sometimes wondered how she coped with her family and job. So, one big THANK YOU, to one and all, for the laughs, the tears, the tiffs and the sheer exuberance of the Wonderbrass experience.

Parallel to all this music making, so much more was going on, but I feel I must concentrate on this one subject, before exploring the complexities of the sporting activities. I simply can not remember the first discovery of Café Jazz in Cardiff, but since then, it has become my Mecca and second home. I even dared on one of my earliest visits to the regular Jam nights, to join in with some poor unsuspecting musician. My performance hardly set the world alight, in fact, it had more chance of clearing the place of all its customers. The performance was noticed by one gentleman, who happened to be an old friend from my days working at Butlins in Barry. Peter Wilson had the misfortune of being at the bar that night, and later admitted to me that he had commented to a friend that, whoever was playing that trombone, was either clueless or a genius; he was right on the first assessment.

So many nights of music have flowed over and through my head at this venue, but here is not the place to discuss the merits or otherwise of the music, but to try and convey the impact the collective experiences have had on me. In particular the people involved, either as listeners, or musicians, who have enriched my experiences in my fifth and sixth decades.

So many extraordinary people would never have crossed my path, had it not been for my interest in music at this venue. Marcin Wright, Peter Wilson, the O'Connors, Ian Pool, Tom Lloyd and Howard, Jim Barber, the Jones's (several of these), Roger Warburton, Eirig and so many more, to say nothing of the staff, especially Lisa, Mireille and her fellow workers.

The unpredictability of music, particularly jazz, is what attracts me, although I have to admit, that it really is only live music that keeps me coming back for more. This applies to the classics, but in a slightly different way, for I enjoy the consistency of the classics, because they are set in stone and are constant to me. On the other hand, jazz is an expression of life to me, and should reflect the feelings of the performer, translating sadness, happiness, anger and all the human emotions into the language of sound, this being the emotion of that moment only.

While this torrent of music was invading my world, many other distractions were burning a tattoo into my brain, but to oscillate back and forth, would be difficult for me, let alone the reader. So Table Tennis must wait, as does the Cricket, even though I feel that they are both inextricably linked to the final conclusions, along with the meditation sessions.

I received word one day of a new venue for the jazz enthusiast, somewhere on the Riverside of town; it turned out to be the Riverbank Hotel, soon to become a regular haunt on Wednesdays and Fridays. The unique Cellar bar had thick pillars punctuating the view and the sounds, yet it felt to me like home, with many an evening sipping my lemonade alongside Ray and sometimes no one else.

In charge were two of the most dedicated people I have ever had the pleasure to meet, they were the A&B of jazz, and still are. Alistair and Brenda shine like a beacon on the world of jazz in South Wales, promoting, without gain for themselves, giving young and old alike a chance to perform in order to develop their skills in front of an audience. Their non-judgemental approach has always impressed me, simply giving their time, year in year out, in their desire to offer the chance to anyone to make their own kind of music.

This was the venue, where I joined a certain Dave Morrow in a rendering of 'Blue Bossa'. A night when I had been pushed in a new direction, not of my choosing, but ultimately proving to be beneficial to all except two rather special persons. They have, however, proved to be strong individuals, and I am confident, they will succeed in their own way, under their own steam.

That 'Blue Bossa' turned out to be a very personal statement by me, blowing some of my sadness into the night, heralding a new day. Although it was all so personal, I felt it was the kind of event that could be portrayed through the medium of music, dissipating much of the heartache, without involving others. On this occasion however, it was picked up by Brenda, as she later admitted to me.

Music was becoming an outlet to calm the frustrations of everyday chores, along with the challenges in its execution, it was becoming a language without swear words, a notion that pleases me no end. Soon I felt the need to attempt new experiences in jazz by joining a class run by Paula Gardner, who had a knack of relaxing her students in order that they would play uninhibited by their shyness or lack of confidence. It was here that I first dared to sing, instead of playing a number I did not know well enough to play on the trombone. I did not know the words, so I scatted in a little used version of Russian. To be honest, it was a load of gobbledegook, but apparently sounded somewhat convincing.

This idiosyncratic technique was used on one particular occasion to good effect, when we were asked to play for a seventieth birthday, for some guy in Dinas Powys, by Dave Western from Wonderbrass. We were a mixed crew of varying abilities, getting together a couple of hours before the performance to put together a gig list.

The rehearsal was an unmitigated disaster, leading us to believe it would not be a night to remember. Not so; we did a couple of reasonable numbers, apparently appreciated by the generally aged audience, before a lady was insisting on doing a number with us namely "I did it my way". She certainly did, as for most of the number, the microphone was not switched on, and the audience watched the old dear mime into a microphone. They were spared these captivating sounds, while we in the band could hear the subtle variations in pitch and tempo all too clearly.

There was a lull in proceedings, and Dave asked us for some ideas, so I said I would do my version of a Russian 'Summertime'. Dave agreed and took a side seat out of sight of the band. The audience were captivated at the Valley boy's mastery of the lilting language of Eastern Europe, I clearly recall the serious looks on the front row listeners, which had also been noticed by Dave. He, however, was about to explode into hysterics, for reasons you will have to ask him about. This situation was noticed by a couple of the partners of the band members, sitting at the back; they witnessed Dave losing control, and slowly sliding down the wall he was leaning against, collapsing in a hysterical heap on the floor.

Had I been aware of these goings on at the time, I would never have completed the number. Luckily it was only later I found out about these reactions. The audience seemed oblivious of anything untoward, and showed their appreciation in the usual way. This spurred us on to do a version of 'Blue Monk' with Stuart, myself, Simon and the rest of the gang, completing a memorable night never to be repeated (or will it?).

I feel I should explain here, that the technique of mimicking a foreign language, had begun many years earlier, probably as early as 1957, when I met many of the Hungarian refugees in and around the Pontypridd area. I found their sounds very pleasing, so eventually began using the odd word or two, or rather the odd sound or two, as I did not pretend to understand the languages.

The Russian sound was special to me, with the strange echo effect that seemed to emanate from a cavity in the mouth. It seemed to me that they had marbles rolling around in their mouths as they spoke. The earliest recollection of using the foreign language sound-alike, was when I was approached by a street salesman. I remember looking at him with a distant look on my face, and when he stopped, I blurted out a short string of total nonsense that sounded Eastern European, he immediately gave up, moving on to some other target.

As for the episodes of singing in this medium, it has always been done without any serious intent, as I find singing requires a persona alien to me, though I do not readily take to singers in general, I have to admit a certain admiration of their courage, if not the abilities.

Wonderbrass performances were at vastly different locations, from theatres, to football clubs, to student unions, to say nothing of freezing cold open air marches. One such marching gig was at Ely in Cardiff, where we gathered at one location and parked our vehicles, played on the march to another location, and returned the mile or so to the start point to collect our vehicles. Some of us were offered a lift back to the start by the police, this entailed cramming into the back of a small Black Maria. Our instruments on our laps, or in my case, upright in front of me, we set off through the Housing Estate feeling like criminals off to the Nick. Suddenly we were all hurled to the very low roof, when the driver decided to take off over a speed bump. The amusement for the driver was short lived as the mouthpiece of my trombone slammed into my mouth, disturbing one tooth, and cutting my lip. I am pleased to say it is the only occasion I have used this form of transport, and strongly recommend against it for anyone else.

At an occasion in West Wales, when we were to play in a football clubhouse, as part of a festival, we set up to a non-existing audience. Apparently, messages were sent by the organizers to drum up some kind of an audience, resulting in some local council members and some officials turning up, numbering seventeen or so in total.

They were very subdued, although I noticed some foot-tapping going on with one girl in particular, so I decided to leave the small stage area, and get some dancing going. Soon we had everyone tripping the light fantastic, with the gig turning out well, after a very dodgy start. I did not play much on that particular gig, but got lots of dancing practice.

I had so many good times with the band, including playing alongside musicians like Jason Yarde and Claude Deppa. However, I must admit, that from a personal viewpoint, I put Rob Smith above all others that I have heard. This is, in part, because of his consistency, along with his perseverance in putting up with us amateurs, seemingly without reaction. For anyone who has not experienced the buzz, of playing music with a bunch of other musicians, I can only say, try it, for only then will you understand the rush you can experience.

Rush, would not be close to describing one of the final gigs I played with Wonderbrass. It was at The Globe in Albany Road in Cardiff. It was a charity gig for Mind and there was a mighty crowd intent on enjoying themselves. We were not in particularly good form, but it is a strange phenomenon, that when a crowd reacts to a band, there is a transfer of energy that sparks more of an atmosphere, resulting in a memorable outcome.

The stage was very small, giving little room for the large turnout that night, but elbow to elbow, we managed a few numbers without too much trouble. We then came to a song that included some vocals, with Fran and Jenny making their way to the central microphone. This meant squeezing past the Trombone section, very nice, leaving us trapped between them and the small raised area for the drums and guitars. Here I must explain that my vertigo was particularly bad in dark or confined spaces, and this was both. The girls were well into their singing, when their dancing was forcing me backwards into a space that did not exist. Something had to give, and as I turned to try to hold on to something to avoid getting in their way, I lost it.

The result was a slow motion domino effect, first I gently tumbled backwards, carefully avoiding the drum kit, but bringing down John the guitarist. The two of us were on our backs, feet in the air, trapped amongst our colleagues, trying to be inconspicuous, both unhurt apart from our pride. Somehow we regained our feet, and like all good troopers, continued to the end of the number, without too many even noticing the misdemeanour.

I managed a solo that night, and got a feeling that it may be time to make way for some new blood, the gig having given one of the best reactions I had experienced with the band. The reaction of the crowd got me considering my own reactions, along with recollections of my memories from their side. There was a euphoric reaction to many events I had attended, regardless of the quality of the perform-ance, leading me to consider the possibility, that "All" is in the eye of the beholder.

Time had run out for me at Wonderbrass. With the new challenge I had begun, I felt clearly the time was right to call it a day. It was one of those moments of certainty, and with a genuine big thank you to Rob and Mark the drummer, I took to the outside looking in. The new challenge was to learn to read music, in order to play with the City Of Cardiff Training Band. This task is ongoing, trying to remember the few things I had learned all those years ago in school.

Dave Howard leads the group, and with considerable help from the other Trombones, especially Josh, I muddle through rehearsals somehow. The discipline required gives the project a new dimension for me. We shall wait and see if it bears fruit. I must also mention here that it was a certain Mr. Dave Weston that first pushed me in this direction. For this, thanks from myself, and apologies to those who now have to endure my playing.

I have considered here mentioning the names of many of the students at the Royal College of Music in Cardiff, who entertain so many of us punters in Café Jazz, along with many other venues. I feel it would be unfair on others, if I were to name names, and so I shall place on record here, that they have, are, and I am sure will continue to give massive pleasure through their inventive playing, to one and all.

It must not go unmentioned that tutors at the College are to be applauded for their obvious contributions to these young musicians' progress. Their dedication to these students provides us listeners with a seemingly never ending stream of musical talents, making Cardiff a very fortunate area to live in at this time.

Cricket, Table Tennis & Frenchay Hospital

Now I must return to the early nineties, for at the same point of introduction to the music scene, I also began an interest in new sports, namely table tennis, and cricket. How the table tennis started I simply cannot recall, but I was soon involved in local leagues, playing in the Aberdare and Cardiff Leagues. I began getting great benefits from the new activity, as this did not seem to be so severe on my back, as badminton had been. One character I met early on was Jack Bullock, who played with the YMCA team in Pontypridd. He was a Welsh International, and well remembered my brother Bryan, who had also been an international many years earlier.

For any of my opponents who dislike the effects of the Kill-Spin rubbers I use on my bat, I can here state that it was Jack who watched my style of play, and recommended this particular rubber for my bat. That same rubber still teases some of my opponents, although I feel the same about some of the rubbers I play against. This introduction to a new sport for me, started up friendships in a new field, adding to the mixture of friends made from my other interests. There were to be even more additions, in the other new sport introduced at the same time, CRICKET.

It was late one afternoon, towards the end of summer, when Dennis Pounder came into my shop, and asked if I would play cricket that evening in Hopkinstown. I explained I did not play cricket, and never had, but he insisted that did not matter as it was just a friendly, and most of the participants were of the same ilk. I eventually agreed, borrowing kit from somewhere, turning up not really knowing what to expect. We bowled first, and I was given one over that was reasonably successful, taking one wicket for one run.

The bowling had not exactly lit my fire, but when I donned the batting kit, I really came to life, marching out to set the world alight. I had watched the previous batsmen fail miserably, and I thought, "how difficult can this be?". The bowler was hardly a Michael Holding, and I prepared to launch him into the river, a mere 30 yards away, no thought of defence, it had to go.

It was the first ball I had ever faced, and the memory of that delivery is still clear in my mind. It bounced short of a length, a foot outside the off stump, rising to a manageable height to be dispatched. Smack; the sound of leather on willow, was like hearing a symphony orchestra for the first time, or witnessing your first great sunset, or the meeting with your first girlfriend. It was inevitably the start of something meaningful, as the ball sped towards the boundary, four feet off the ground, travelling like a missile, I watched, awestruck as it was intercepted by the chest of the mid-off fielder, who staggered backwards with the sheer force of the projectile, clinging on, to bring my short visit to an end. The feeling then, was one of amazement, walking back to the clubhouse, looking at the bat, smiling, at the sheer joy of striking the ball off the middle of the bat.

The die was set, there would be no turning back, there had to be more of this feeling, and very soon, but that proved more difficult than I had imagined. I was 53 years old – too old to learn new tricks, or so most seemed to think when I tried to join clubs in the area. If it had not been for one man, I may not have got a chance to delve into the intricacies of this game of all games. It is a game that demands all the ingredients for living: respect, patience, perseverance and so much more, but most of all, as in life, there must be total respect.

Tony Hallet was to be the man. He set me on a path to become a cricketer of sorts, inviting me to net with his beloved Pontypridd Cricket Club. It was to become a roller-coaster ride with multiple influences, both in terms of sport and life. My selfishness up till then had not been too obvious to myself, but this amazing game taught me so much over the next years, leading me into new concepts of 'Self'.

The earliest lesson was learnt from a very good batsman who had faced me in an early net practice. I had, by accident, bowled just one good line and length ball that had undone his defence, and we were soon in a team playing an early season friendly. I was as green as they come, but wildly enthusiastic, itching to get started. I was asked to get the pads on to bat very soon, I was all fingers and thumbs trying to rush the preparations, and it was he who took me aside, to calm the brain, giving me some obvious advice, but only in hindsight. He said, "Walk purposefully, and confidently, bat under arm, looking as though you know all there is to know about batting." A simple lesson, yet one that can be translated to most of life's challenges.

I did not last long at the crease that day, but that lesson was well learnt, standing me in good stead ever since, both on and off the field. Soon, my newly acquired whites were in constant use. I became a regular in the 3rd XI, and made a whole new batch of friends, both in our club and our opponents, a trait familiar to cricket and other sports.

Tony Hallet was, and still is, held in the highest esteem, by myself, as well as his club mates. He always insists on fair play, allied to total respect, for the game, the players, and the officials. His prowess as a captain stands at the top of my list, along with Jonathan Morgan who will feature later in this section. What stands out so strongly in my recollections is their man management skills, proving to me their constant thought for all the team, not just the stars.

A distinct event highlights this, when in a game at Pontypridd, one of the opposition was given out by the umpire, for LBW. As the batsman left the field the fielders gathered to celebrate, but a couple of us stated that we were sure the batsman had edged the ball before hitting his pad. After asking if we were sure, he told the umpire to call back the batsman to continue his innings. Anyone who has played this exclusive game will know how rare this kind of action is, but what effect it has on others in the team, especially the batsman.

I have done little captaincy in my cricket career so far, but here I admit to at least three occasions when I have made the same judgement, much to the pleasure of the recipients, and the displeasure of the bowler. Having been the bowler on at least one of these occasions, the disappointment soon reverts to acceptance, with a strong feeling of fairness, hoping one day, one might be the recipient of such an action.

I was driving to one match accompanied by two of my fellow players, Chris and Tom. Travelling towards Barry I did not see a cat run under the car from the side. It was badly injured. In the mirror I could see that the poor animal was beyond repair, but still alive. Very quickly I realised that the only humane action was to put the animal out of its misery, and so I reversed hoping to do the right thing quickly and efficiently. At the third attempt I was successful, if I can put it this way; but by this time I was very upset, and could not immediately continue the journey. Chris Richards had abilities to defuse situations, and as we had all seen the cat's movements after the first contact, he quickly said "haven't you seen a cat break-dance before?". It had been the second occasion within two weeks that such an incident had happened to me. I am glad to report, it has not been repeated since.

Much has been written about this exclusive game, imitating life itself, with all its ups, downs, twists and turns, culminating in a strange satisfaction at the end of the game. The nearlys, the maybes along with the downright never weres, all add to the fascination, or frustrations, this game has to offer.

I can barely scratch the surface of the various games that highlight my rather obvious infatuation for cricket, so I will randomly quote from the store of facts, as I remember them. Sammy was captain of Ponty 3rd XI quite early in my career, with a tendency to bat stepping across his crease with his front foot, leaving a gap for the ball to sneak through. Regrettably, it was a trait he never mastered. But in a game on a small ground south of Ebbw Vale, his time came to show he could master this slight chink in his armour, producing a superb innings of 112.

The sight of his pleasure-filled expression as he left the field, showed me how important the simple things are in life, reinforcing my conviction, that all of us will experience the great highs, as well as the lows, leaving us all as part of this great bringing together of experience called a life. In this same game, another incident focused on the less than savoury aspect of some who grace this earth. It was our opponents' innings, and I was bowling at a senior member of their side. He was very vocal, both to his own team members, their umpires, as well as trying to boss us as bowlers. I had a very definite appeal for LBW, turning to the very young umpire, standing bemused, not knowing what to do. As if in slow motion, he was starting to raise his finger to confirm the out decision, when the batsman stormed up the strip, wildly remonstrating that it could not have been out, telling the frightened young lad to reverse his decision.

Happily, this kind of unacceptable behaviour is very rare, so if the person in question reads this, I trust you have learned a lesson by simply looking at your own actions. The result of the game is really quite irrelevant. I have to admit that the only memory of this game was the positive one of Sammy's century, with the second memory only re-emerging while telling the first story.

Sammy's faith in my bowling was frequently pointed out to me. One occasion put me to the test in no uncertain terms. The game was against Barry, at a small ground above Aberdare. Barry's captain was my first encounter against a formidable cricketer, and one of many dedicated cricket fanatics. Glan is another in the mould of the Tony Hallets of this wonderful world of cricket, fair and respectful of all on the field of play. Sammy had asked if I would bowl the full complement that day, as he had little bowling. I remember the result, my figures, and nothing else of that day's fun, which for me is quite unusual, as I rarely look at the details of the game just played, but simply check where the next game is going to be.

In the forty over game, I bowled non-stop from start to finish, ending with figures of 20 overs, four or five maidens, five wickets for 42 runs. Why I should remember this is probably because on return to our meeting place later that evening in the Maltsters in Pontypridd, I was asked for my figures by Tony, to be scolded for allowing 42 runs to be scored!

I will here thank Sammy for another of his regular considerations towards me, as he batted me frequently at six, seven or eight, giving me a chance to enjoy the delights of that art, as well as my bowling. Thank you, Sammy and all the lads of those years in the 3rds.

Our home fixtures at that juncture were at the University fields in Treforest, regrettably not in existence any more. It was here that one of my most pleasurable innings took place. It was a fixture I had said I would not be able to start, but would turn up when I had completed a wedding booking. I duly arrived at about 3.00pm to find a somewhat dejected Ponty side, batting on 26 runs for five wickets. As I turned the corner into view, it was urgently gestured across the field to "get my whites on", get padded up, and get ready to help save a serious humiliation.

It was Ebbw Vale again, a very fine club with a great tradition. I prepared for the rear guard action making up the full complement of eleven. At 29 runs another wicket fell, six down now and facing a serious humiliation, in cricket terms. As I made my way to the middle, I was met by the formidable figure of Jazza, a six foot plus man, with considerable muscle power to dispatch a cricket ball many a mile. His main problem was the quick single or leisurely two, to say nothing of the impossible three. We set about putting to right the sad sight on the scoreboard, slowly edging our way towards respectability, with much jeering from our fallen colleagues, when a single was turned down, along with encouragement, when Jazza lofted a six, or hammered a four through the covers.

I was intent on staying there, as Jazza was in full swing, hitting regular boundaries, taking his tally upwards towards the magical three figures. While I tried to give him the strike to further our cause, I had to endure many declined runs, and I crawled towards a quarter century. One of their bowlers was approaching his last few deliveries, and already had four wickets, needing that one more to make it a

'Fifor'. I was facing these last few deliveries, and as he was their premier bowler, we wanted to see him off, to give us a chance to move our score quicker against their lesser bowlers.

As if in slow motion, his medium paced delivery near the end of his spell, came towards me outside the off stump, his expectation of that elusive fifth wicket burning a hole in my bat, hoping for some indiscretion on my part. I reached forward, bat and pad together, (O.K. boys, those who know my batting prowess will know that is unlikely), allowing the ball to sail majestically into the keeper's gloves, having passed my good self with some minor noise attributable to an unknown source.

The bowler leapt some feet in the air, turning for the reaction of our umpire. The pregnant two-second pause was a heart stopping moment for both of us, and it was to be my delight and his despair, that the umpire shook his head. To this day, I can not decide finally whether I did nick that ball, or whether it was a pad brush, or some other noise, but one thing I am sure of, is that the bowler was in no doubt, and showed considerable displeasure for some time after the incident. If I did nick the ball, I hereby apologise to that bowler, but I was not sure, consequently leaving it to the umpire. This occurrence has made me an advocate of always walking if I am sure I am out, regardless of the consequences. I firmly believe it to be the only way to show total respect to all.

Jazza failed to reach the magical three figures that day, and we duly lost the game, but the 115 partnership lives on in my memory, as one of many incidents that make the game what it is. One other thing I learned that day, was the value of encouragement in times of pain or discomfort, as Jazza confided in me many times during that innings, that his ability to bat on through exhaustion, needed constant denials from me, keeping him focused on the job in hand. To his credit, he came through with flying colours. Why do I remember one shot from that innings of mine, when I hooked a short ball for four, past backward-square-leg? Who knows.

What is the worst way of getting out for a batsman? It has to be the fluke run-out. Only once in my short career has this fate fallen on me, and I trust, never again. It was a tour match somewhere in Dorset or Devon, and there had been a mix up with a venue, with a lucky break by myself, finding the ground just in time to save an embarrassing non-appearance. Through an administrative error, we went initially to the wrong ground, so I had toured off to find the other ground and ring back to the squad my findings.

For my initiative I was asked to open the innings, accepting with some relish. I faced two or three balls scoring a magnificent two with a late-cut to third man, then watched my partner face the first ball of the next over. The next ten seconds lives on in my mind, like a Charlie Chaplin silent movie, only in slow motion, as opposed to the stuttering style of the great comedian. The bowler was not in the spring of youth, and I suspect, had not loosened himself adequately for the job in hand. His first ball was driven straight back, gently towards the bowler, in the air, about a foot off the ground, in reasonable catching height. In that fleeting moment, I saw the bowler consider stooping to catch the ball, realise it would hurt to bend, leaving the ball to take its course. I was already a yard out of my crease, and watched in disbelief, as the ball brushed his trouser leg, careering into my stumps.

I learned absolutely nothing from this experience, except how to laugh when you feel like screaming, stamping, or burying your head in your hands. "Such is life".

Up to this point, I had only played for Pontypridd, but as we meet new people, we tend to seek new challenges, taking us to pastures new. This was the case when I moved to play for Creigiau, where I knew one of their members through my table tennis. Trevor Fox had indicated I might get regular games at a level that suited my abilities. I have always maintained my association with Pontypridd, watching the results with as much interest as ever, occasionally turning out in friendlies, for the team that gave me my first taste of the game.

Creigiau turned out to be the ideal club on more than one account, as it was emerging from the friendly cricket, towards league status. The enthusiasm of the members there was to be admired, and the challenges many and varied, giving me the feeling that my new interest in the game would match the emergence of their club. It took little time for me to settle in, although it soon became apparent that I was to be labelled only as a bowler. This meant batting at number eleven in most games, losing the little ability I had procured in my cricket up till then.

Our daughter Katy had shown an interest in making teas for the occasional game, choosing accidentally to be the said tea-lady at my first hat-trick performance. She had no interest in the game itself, and was sitting reading, while waiting for the tea-time work. I was bowling from the road end of the pitch, and was pleased to find myself with two consecutive wickets. Anyone who plays the game, and is a specialist bowler, knows the tension that grows as the possibility of the hat-trick presents itself, with anxiety increasing as you wait for that next batsman to make his way out. It was the eighth time I had been on the hat-trick, all previous occasions ending in a poor delivery giving little chance of success.

This was to be the one to break the mould, so I deliberately calmed down, giving the situation the consideration it deserved. I paused quietly at the end of my usual short run up, determined to simply bowl my stock off-spin delivery. As has happened on several occasions since, I released the ball, knowing it was to be a successful delivery, with the inevitable clatter of the ball breaking the stumps.

The celebrations were the usual dancing down the pitch, with back slapping and handshakes all round from your team-mates. I have never come to terms with the feeling that constantly comes to me as the batsman walks off. I feel bad for taking their enjoyment, spoiling their day; perhaps an admission I should have kept to myself. On this occasion, we left the field for the tea-break, to be confronted by my somewhat embarrassed daughter asking why I had behaved in the way I had. I informed her that I had just taken a hat-trick, to which she replied, "is that good?". No comment.

Here I must document the onset of the medical problem, namely, the tumour, that afflicted me at around this period. I have debated for some days, as to whether I should include something so personal and seemingly irrelevant. I have come to the conclusion, that without the story itself, I could not hope to explain the consequences or effects of this period on my life so far.

The earliest incident that I can recall, was at a cricket match, chasing a ball to the boundary, I went to stop the ball, and stubbed my right foot, almost going head over heels into a hedge. This slowly became a common occurrence just while walking, linked with calf cramps, especially at night. These progressed to burning sensations, mainly in the left leg, very gradually getting stronger over the next year or so. Finally, one of those certain moments occurred, a realisation that something was wrong. I recall a strong fear flooding my senses, along with a determination to get it sorted. It was not that easy though, as investigations showed nothing specific, while the condition continued to intensify.

Finally, I went for a second MRI scan to Frenchay Hospital in Bristol, where they scanned the full length of my spine. Half way through, a lady interrupted the procedure to inform me in just four words, "we've found a growth". My mind had discounted this possibility as some kind of defence, but this hit me like a sledge-hammer. Further scans were done while I tried to assess the possibilities, and having only these four words to understand my predicament, I came to some bad conclusions.

The journey home was not the most enjoyable I have ever taken, so I phoned a cricket friend who is a no-nonsense bloke, and arranged to meet him before returning home to my family. Chris listened to the revelations, including my reaction when I stopped for petrol at a Motorway Services. I had filled the car with fuel, and entered the shop to pay. The young girl asked the pump number, casually asking "how are you?", or something similar, and I burst into uncontrollable tears.

Chris's reaction to this story was instant and poignant, defusing my fears immediately. "She must have thought it was your last £20" he said smiling, breaking me away from the self pity that was swamping my mind. So many people have to face such situations daily, that it is difficult to comprehend the turmoil that must affect everybody at some time in their lives.

That was the turning point in my little fight, for within weeks I was summoned to the same Frenchay Hospital for an operation, trying to be positive about the whole thing. As would be the case with most in this situation, there are doubts or fears creeping into your mind, although I used my own technique to allay such thoughts, pouring energy flows from the mind down the neck into my back. It is more than positive thinking, more the use of the dormant power of the brain, something I feel is in everyone, though not generally utilised.

I met the surgeon the night before the op., a Mr Ian Pople, who arrived as I was practicing spinning a cricket ball, keeping my fingers supple ready for future work on the field. No, not up and down the ward, just in the air and back into my palm. I recall he used few words, rather quietly making some ink marks at the area to be worked on the next day, assuring me all would be well, and left.

A vivid image embedded in my mind, is my daughter Helga's smiling face waving a farewell from the end of the ward, saying "see you tomorrow".

That evening I chatted to several of the other occupants on the ward, in particular a young sixteen year old, and a 50 plus man who turned out to be a very brave chap, facing the almost certain bad end to his fight with cancer of the spine. His fortitude impressed me no end, making me realise again how lucky I was. His solid, sad, yet somehow peaceful attitude, gave me great strength for the minor skirmish I was about to face.

The big sleep lasted from 8.45am until well into the evening, drifting back into dreamy consciousness around 8.30pm, missing a waiting friend, Richard (Trumpet) who had come to see me. The morphine kept me peaceful through the night, but morning brought the reality firmly home to me. The date was the 1st January, the start of a new year, full of new possibilities after the running repairs to my back.

8.30am: Mr Pople called to see me. This amazing man had worked all day, on New Year's Eve, done another operation after mine, and was back on New Year's Day to check on his patients. The hint of a smile put me immediately at ease, while he asked me to wiggle my toes, successfully I must add, and he departed with the words I had hoped to hear. "Don't worry, you will play cricket again this year."

I often reminisce on the few days spent at that Hospital, the West Indian Auxiliary Nurse who was so patient and supportive, helping me back on my feet. The gent I have previously mentioned, as well as the young lad who had had major surgery to remove a tumour from his brain. He was a bright and cheerful boy with positive vibes, dealing so well with his fight, making fun of the experience he had after the surgery. It seems the morphine had prompted hallucinations, seeing strange monsters walking along the rail around his bed. All around me were these fantastic people, all with their own particular struggles, giving strength to each other.

In the quiet moments, I persevered with my own healing process, pouring the energy from the brain down my back, like waves breaking on a beach, a process I have endeavoured to adapt, to sending this energy to others.

I was released, a few days later, to be driven home by Romela, who is one of the best drivers I have known, although I must admit that every bump in the road that day, tested my resolve to the limit. Reaching home highlighted the usual recovery problems everybody encounters in these circumstances, with sleep a difficult operation due to the position of the surgery. The tensions built up physically, as movements were very difficult, resulting in a build up of physical and mental tensions that had to be released.

This happened some days after my release from hospital, in a most unexpected way. We had decided to watch a DVD, itself a rare occurrence for us all together. It was an American film I had not heard of, namely *Field Of Dreams*. During that viewing, I experienced several uncharacteristic explosions of emotion, bursting into tears on at least five occasions. My son Richard was very supportive throughout, and I am convinced that the outpouring of energy hastened my recovery, releasing all the pent up mental stress, as well as the physical.

More Cricket

It was a very short time before I started work again, along with a desire to restart my cricketing career, trying the odd net practice, before the April start to the season. It was not long before I was back in the swing, teasing the odd batsman with my slow non-spin.

A charity match was arranged to raise money for the Ward in Frenchay Hospital, bringing in some £700. The match itself was played on a small ground inside the grounds of the Hospital with an appearance by a family member of Neil Jenkins, one of the legends of the rugby fraternity in Pontypridd, Neil still very busy with his rugby at that time. His brother-in-law also brought the blow-up sheep as an extra fielder, which caused some amusement, but proved to be somewhat ineffective at square-leg. I believe it was the first time I played in the same team with the Morgans of Creigiau, an association that has grown to being almost family a decade later. Peter, Jonathan, Tom and a very young Andrew were all involved, along with mum Caroline, who would have played also if the need had arisen.

Also in our team was Tony Hallet, the larger than life character who lights up any gathering of sportsmen. We were to take on a hospital based team with some very able cricketers, none more so than Mr Ian Pople, the surgeon that got into my spine to sort things out. He was now about to get into my mind on the cricket field, his considerable cricket skills disposing of my batting attempt, with a fine throw and run-out from the deep.

The result was a distant second place for us, but that was irrelevant, as the thank you to the Hospital staff was the only reason for the event, the memory of which is a constant reminder to me, of the wonderful work they do for so many.

My passion for the game of cricket had given me a reputation, that of a mercenary, offering to play anywhere, at the drop of a hat, for anyone. For this I make no apology, as it has resulted in a great variety of experiences, with, and against, so many teams, meeting a wide range of individuals, from all sections of our society. Most prominent in this respect, would be our Asian friends, with whom I feel most at home, perhaps partly because my previous travels through their countries enabled me to build a bond in my own mind with these passionate and devout people.

These words may give the impression that I have some sort of religious sympathy with their cultures, but this would be far from the truth, as I have long rejected all of the religions that I have encountered. I favour of the individual, along with his or her Karma. All I can relate, is that when I show total respect for my fellow man, our differences diminish, and the more respect there is.

Veejay, Girish and Sameep, have all been part of the cricket at Creigiau, all becoming friends over the last years, all contributing to the scene, both on and off the cricket field. Two of these three were involved in one of the most memorable games I have ever had the privilege to be a part of. I was taking photographs at a wedding on this particular day, and was not able to play. However I had said that I would attend, as soon as I completed the said work.

I arrived at the ground in my suit at around 3.45pm. to find our team batting. Peter Morgan and Girish were at the crease, and I simply stood by the car, some distance from the clubhouse. Llantwit Major was the venue, Jonathan Morgan was captain, and it was a beautiful day. As I stood watching from the car park, a very young Dan Pearson raced towards me around the boundary, calling something while waving vigorously. The message was to, "get the whites on, get the pads on, ASAP."

Not being one to turn any game down, I obliged, finding myself joining Peter at the crease, with the score on around 60 runs for seven wickets. We were in a bit of a predicament, considering Llantwit Major were a very reasonable side, with sufficient batting strength to easily reach 150 to 200 runs. We reached 86 runs for seven or eight wickets, expecting a swift conclusion after tea. Jonathan had other ideas, trying hard to instil some positive thoughts in us all. However, I do not believe there were any of us that thought this one could be saved, but, sport has a way of very occasionally throwing up the unexpected. This was to be one such occasion, as the opposition confidently took to the field, utterly sure of themselves. Already celebrating inside, they set about the seemingly straightforward task ahead.

I recall the definite feeling at the start of their innings, that it was just a matter of time, for on a scale of one to ten, our chance of a win was zero. When they were 35 for no wicket, zero was down to minus zero, yet Jonathan continued with a confidence he alone was able to muster. One great catch by Oliver Bowker at mid-off above his head, tipped the sliding scale back to zero, but the batters looked confident, despite losing one or two more wickets, they were moving inexorably towards their goal.

The scoring slowed to a crawl, as they crept towards their target, but still there was only a one in ten chance of success, when a couple more wickets fell, boosting our feelings to three in ten. Most of their batsmen were now getting a little nervous, all except one of their young guns who was supremely confident, showing a considerable desire to finish things off.

Jonathan and I got together to share some thoughts, both agreeing that a chance had to be taken, in that we would try the young leg-spinner Dan Pearson. They were now a mere ten runs short of their target, with four wickets remaining, the next two overs were a revelation to us, as the first batsman danced down the wicket to put the leggy out of the ground, only to miss the ball and get himself stumped by a youthful Owain Jones, followed by two more over-confident batsmen getting bowled. The situation was now seven runs needed, 9 wickets down, the young good batsman on strike, waiting for his moment of glory.

Jonathan threw the ball to me to try and work some magic. They had several overs to get the runs, but I felt the young man was in a hurry to show his talents. First ball, no run, second ball was dispatched for four. His demeanour was now one of total confidence as he faced me down the wicket. I seem to remember looking straight at the lad, smiling as I did so, delaying my next delivery to adjust the field, giving him some easy options to get single runs. He fell for it, gently paddling the ball to fine leg, allowing him an easy single. I am sure that as he ran the length of the wicket for that single, it dawned on him that he had made a fatal error of judgment, placing the number eleven batsman to face the bowling.

As all the fielders closed in, putting pressure on the number eleven batter, I clearly recall the look on his face as I prepared to deliver the next ball, that one second, looking at him before the delivery, told me that it only had to be a straight ball, to give us the most unlikely of victories. It was another example of a slow-motion certainty, for as the ball left my hand, I knew the outcome would be success as the ball pitched, turned a little, missed the cross-the-line bat, clattering into the stumps.

In that moment I had a feeling of immense elation, along with genuine thoughts for the young batsman that had narrowly failed to secure the win. The celebration that followed was a one off, for I have never before been a part of such a team effort, with every single player in our side being an equal part of the success. Of course the Captain must take top spot, although I am sure he would have denied such recognition, insisting that it was a combined effort, with no individual taking the honours. It must be a peculiarity of my make-up, that constantly makes me look at the other side of situations, wondering how this event affected that young batsman, and whether he had learnt anything from the experience.

So many experiences spring to mind in this period, that may, or may not have affected the way I think towards my fellow man, so I will try to isolate those that I feel have done so. In cricket, simple things, like honouring with respect all umpires' decisions, something that took many a long "Tea-pot" stance to eliminate from my playing reactions. The adding of "Sir", to all my "Howzat" appeals, with always an acceptance of any refusal with dignity. Personally, I have found that this attitude brings rewards far greater than should sometimes be, as respect is often returned with interest. May I add here, that that is not the reason I take this stance, but that it is an unsolicited result of my attitude.

A lesson learnt quite late in my cricket career, was the way I would talk to a batsman after he had been dismissed. This was always done out of respect, often praising them for a good innings, or an unfortunate dismissal. On one occasion it nearly caused an incident, when the batsman on his way back to the pavilion took great umbrage to my comment of "well batted". Dave was a very intense cricketer, who always gave his all, especially with his running between wickets. Unfortunately, on this occasion, it caused his downfall, being run-out trying to scamper an extra run for his team. He wrongly thought I was being facetious, and reacted loudly causing the odd verbal retorts. I have since learned the golden rule of "do not ever speak to a batsman after being dismissed, either as player or supporter".

As in life, the best intentions are sometimes misunderstood, causing unnecessary conflicts, often building into situations totally alien to the original word or thought. This brings me to a decision made around the middle part of my short cricket career, where I decided to attend Buddhist Meditation classes. I cannot remember any reason why I did so then, but they have proved invaluable to me. Suma is the lady who led these sessions of meditation, emptying the mind of the negative thoughts, clearing the way for renewed positive, creative thinking.

The sessions I most remember, were at Insole Gardens in Cardiff, where the tranquil surroundings promoted good vibes, although the occasional distraction of some youths staring in the windows would test your ability to concentrate on your meditation to the limit. Meditation is something I had often attempted alone, but it tended to be short lived, whereas in a group, with an experienced leader, meditation was deeper, lasting three or four times the duration.

I suppose I have always been a bit of a loner, but I have to admit that group meditation proved so much more fulfilling, giving me a greater understanding of my fellow man, creating a platform for further understanding of the 'Self', leading to a more balanced perception of others.

I am trying to convey the way so many experiences in my life have led to a huge change in attitude, with a greater emphasis on others, rather than on the little world within my own mind. I have come a long way from Mackintosh Road and the child who started this story. The impermanence of my existence is only beginning to become obvious, as old age takes a grip on the body and the mind. This reinforces my conviction that anger, mistrust, prejudice and the lack of respect for all things living on our amazing planet must be seen by all for what they are. This awareness should spur us to create an alternative to conflict. Otherwise, the next generation will have even greater problems to solve.

South Africa Revisited

As I dodge back and forth, from my short history, to philosophy, and back again, I move to some of the early New Century goings on. My one surviving brother informed me he was returning to the UK with an intention to re-settle here. I was surprised, however, when he talked about the changes he saw here since his last experiences. He had become so used to the different way of life in South Africa that our society had become quite alien to him, resulting in his decision to return after only a year here. Strangely, he informed me that he had a book planned about the psychology of sport, particularly positive approaches in the training of young athletes. Regrettably, he never really got started, having only made some rough notes to that end, before deciding to return to his second set of roots, South Africa, where he continued his passion for bowls and his smoking habit. The latter of these being his eventual downfall, causing two heart attacks, the second of which regrettably ended his life.

Not being able to attend the funeral owing to the great distance, along with work commitments, I sent a synopsis of his early years here in the UK to be read out at his funeral, apparently causing much amusement, breaking the ice at that sombre meeting. I managed to arrange a visit to South Africa, meet his ex-wife, Olivia, his son Gwyn Delano, along with his many friends, some three days after his funeral, being greeted with great enthusiasm by all his friends and relatives.

I must here explain that there were some similarities in appearance between Bryan and myself. This caused more than a little reaction, when I was taken to the Bowls Club where he used to play. That was short lived, and I was soon being treated like a long lost son by the players he had obviously known so well. I had been fortunate enough to have a guide to show me around, in the shape of a close friend of Bryan's, a lad he had worked with in his association with the vertical blind company in Port Elizabeth. He took me to the rugby/cricket stadium opposite the Bowls Club, and made sure I stayed out of trouble during my short visit.

I also wanted to meet Gwyn and Olivia, which I managed to arrange, leading to a stay in a Township overnight, an experience that wakes one up to the huge variations and the continuing rift between groups of people in South Africa. Olivia wanted me to see the results of Bryan's help, placing Gwyn at a great school in Pletenburgh Bay, near the Township where Olivia and Gwyn now lived.

Olivia took me to meet her relatives, and in the car I had hired for the trip, we did the rounds. Olivia was a black South African, obviously proud of her roots, very keen to introduce me to all her cousins, aunts and uncles. She took me to the small house where several of her aunts lived, knocking the door, then pushing it open herself, revealing a passageway leading to a room beyond. This moment was just ten days after Bryan had died, and Olivia called in to her relatives, that there was someone wanting to meet them. As I showed myself at the door, two rather terrified ladies looked at me, and let out a gasp of dismay, thinking Bryan had been reincarnated. It was then that I realised how similar in looks we must have been.

The whole exercise was so worthwhile, as I now feel I understand a little of the world Bryan lived in. Yet, while keeping a fond memory of the short visit I made that June 2004, I cannot find it in me to keep any close contact with his world. Bryan had died aged 65, an apparently fit person, taken early, partly as a result of his smoking habit. A year or two more would have given him the time to write his book.

Ricky Miltz ran the vertical blind company that Bryan had worked for in Port Elizabeth, and, along with so many of his workmates, showed me so much respect, giving me a reassuring view of the kind of life Bryan must have had with these friends around him. One lady along with her boyfriend, whose names escape me, were very kind to me, seeing me to my hotel, and giving me sound advice to keep me safe. This may sound strange in our environment in the UK, but would be appreciated by anyone who has experienced the conditions in SA.

The significance of an incident at this hotel highlights the tensions of their society. When inside the compound of the locked security surround to the hotel, access is by key for residents, with a security bell to be rung for attention by visitors. I was passing the gate inside, when a very aggressive young man outside demanded I open the gate to let him through. I suggested he rang for assistance, as I had no authority to do this. He became most aggressive, eventually producing his own key, and entering the hotel, showing a volatility of character that was most disturbing.

As an outsider, I could see tensions not specifically between blacks and whites, but mainly between the different shades of the mix of Asian, black and white. The level of security that surrounded almost every building was disturbing to say the least, the acceptance of such a standard was even more disturbing to me. All these observations were making me more aware of the need to overcome the divisions of society, in particular the deep prejudices that seem to be reinforced by a media that highlights and distorts actual situations. Everything is in the eye of the beholder, so if we look only at a part of a picture, we can never appreciate the whole.

Back home to a further flavour of cricketing exploits, in particular, a visit to Barry Island, for a mid-week match against Barry Athletic. This is self-indulgent in the extreme, so I shall keep it short. I had bowled three of my four overs, for seventeen runs, with our opponents on 85 for one. At the crease was their best batsman, on 65 runs, showing his intention to score as many runs, as quickly as possible.

My first ball of my fourth over was duly attacked, high into the night sky, straight to a fielder at mid-off. One down, caught by Dave Avery, but what followed in the rest of the over, was more than any of us could have hoped for, for by the end of my fourth over, they were 85 for six. Balls two, three, five and six all claimed wickets, all bowled, causing some consternation in the pavilion, with rapid changes of protective pads and helmets. A t-shirt was later produced with a reference to the internet, i.e. WWW.WW.

An interesting by-product of this fascinating game occurred in a game played at a ground near Ystrad Mynach, some eight miles away. The significance of that distance will become obvious later. The match itself was trundling along. We were bowling, and there was little to remember until one of their batsmen decided to take a risky single off my bowling. Our wicket keeper ran to the ball some three or four yards away, picked up and hurled the same towards the stumps at my end. I was positioned behind the stumps ready to take a run-out, but the ball struck the stumps, diverting into my face, striking me on the eye-brow.

Down I went like a mortally wounded rhino, clutching my face, making an appeal to the umpire for a run-out. Not out, he retorted, but as I revealed my bloody face to the gathered fielders, I realised by their reactions, that I had done some damage to this face of mine.

I left the field of play to try and stem the blood flow, holding the eyebrow together, hoping it would knit together without stitches. So it did, and after rejoining the match to a final conclusion, we enjoyed the usual hospitality, eventually making our way back home.

I was to ferry a couple of the boys home, chatting about the pros and cons of the days activities. It was not until we were half way home that I realised I did not have my driving glasses on, yet in spite of this, I could see very well. I visited the optician soon after, to find that my distant vision had been greatly improved, something the optician did not want to believe. However, I have never worn driving glasses since.

I had become known as the nomad of the cricket scene, always ready for a game for anyone who would offer. The consequence of this attitude, was a change in approach towards sport in general, namely, a non-partisan attachment to any team. This has resulted in a laid back viewing of any match, changing allegiance to the particular situation. At first there were feelings of guilt, but the more the routine went on, the more I felt at ease with the new approach, while still getting enjoyment from the games themselves. All this relates to my changes in philosophical attitudes, from a judgemental mindset, to one of an acceptance that, because I think one way, it does not follow that others will see the same reasoning.

All this now seems so fundamental to me, that I find it hard to envisage the former attitude. This, however, was not the mindset when the second marriage broke up, for I reverted to the old ways of thinking temporarily, initially placing blame as we all seem to do in these situations. This was short lived, as we all have to look hard at ourselves, analysing the facts as honestly as is possible. It soon became apparent to me, that it was an inevitable consequence of circumstances, although I would never have taken that path, rather staying with the situation we had created, making efforts to heal the wounds of that difficult period.

Soon I was to see the situation was better this way, and at a chance meeting of my ex, at a supermarket, who was shopping with her new partner, I reacted in a way, that would have been alien to me a year earlier. Calmly approaching them, I offered my hand to Ian, who had been known to me for some years, to shake hands on the whole affair. He tentatively did so, and I quietly whispered "THANK YOU", and turned and walked on, feeling unbelievably calm, with an easy feeling of closure, and absolutely no ill feeling at all towards anyone. Here I explain, that it was not as a rebuff, but quite simply as a statement to him, that without his interventions, I would still have been in my own unhappy state, making Romela unhappy also. I trust they have a happy existence together, as happy as my situation has also been.

Nepal

Digital photography hit our trade like a tornado, my gut feeling avoided the temptation to invest immediately in this new technology. It proved to be a sound decision, both on cost grounds as well as quality, as the end product did not match the good old negative yet. More than the change of system of recording images, it created a new idea, that photographers could now take as many shots as they wanted, sift through and select at a later date, manipulate the images, and eventually reach a final product that was often gimmicky and distorted. Top quality prints still needed to be done, or the end product would detract from the quality.

All this meant that many budding amateurs suddenly thought they could cash in on an easy option, not realising that it is organisational skills at a wedding that are the essential requirement. For my part, it slowly became a valuable tool of the trade, for I still had the benefit of the old system, which meant I did not have to spend hours in front of a screen, editing the pictures, as I had done most of the work in the camera.

I realise these facts appear to have little to do with what I am trying to convey, but my new found calm has certainly made decision making much clearer, the positive thought processes seemingly leaving a clear path to good decision making.

My brain is starting to hurt with all this philosophical mind-bending, so I shall move on to a trip I made in November 2002 to Kathmandu in Nepal. I was intent on recapturing my youthful days of adventurous wandering, taking the freedom I had been landed with, to try some new lands. I felt drawn to that area, as Tibet had always been on my mind, since hearing the Dalai Lama speak in Cardiff, impressing me with his calm, as well as his total lack of anger towards anyone.

It was very difficult to get into Tibet, although I would have tried if I had been younger. Nepal was a mere stone's throw away, so disregarding the Maoist operations going on there at the time, I was lured to this magical land to savour the culture, along with the glories of the Himalayas. I must admit to being almost as excited as I had been in my youth, but the plane journey somewhat deadened the adventure bit. Once there, it was a different story, with gun-posts at all strategic points adding to the thrill; the delights of the locals' serious, enthralling faces, was yet another eye opener to what we simply do not see in our lives in the UK.

One of my first ports of call was to the Footprint café bar, where all the Everest climbers leave their signatures on carefully preserved boards, including Edmund Hillary and Tenzing Norgay, the Sherpa. Kathmandu was a city like no other I have seen, sprawling across a low lying basin, some 6,000 feet above sea level. At the centre, was a series of temples, dedicated to various Gods, yet it was the people that fascinated me most, with these old buildings taking very much second place. The children were the same as everywhere else, but the middle aged, and the elderly were the gems in this wondrous place, always responding to a greeting of "Namaste", with a smile and a bow of the head in respect. I felt so much at home here, and yet I knew immediately that I could not stay long, the emotion I felt, was sympathy and respect in equal measure, telling me that it was something I could not sustain for long without getting too involved.

In the hotel I was staying at there were very few other guests. The occasional local; respectful, but quiet and reserved, along with one or two fellow travellers, including a wonderful gent from England, on his annual excursion to his favourite destination. We shared long chats about his previous visits, including his long walks through the Himalayas, a tradition he wanted to continue, even though he could no longer manage the difficult terrain. He was well into his seventies, yet retained his youthful outlook, along with a massive respect for the people of Nepal.

It was Diwali, and the days of celebration added to the magical atmosphere throughout the city. The candles flickering through the evening walks gave a warm satisfied glow to the heart. It was a four-day celebration, with a different emphasis for each day. One day was dedicated to the Crow, and people would put food out for the birds, not unlike similar acts by many of us at home. Another day was for the Dogs, a sight that amused me no end, to see dogs with garlands of flowers and painted red spots on their heads, along with a day for the Sacred Cow, with cows similarly adorned. The final day is dedicated to the girls of the family, in relation to the brothers. It was the custom for the boys of the family, to spoil their sisters, doing their work for them for the day, lavishing gifts on them also, in appreciation of their undoubted efforts over the rest of the year.

I had inquired where the cricket ground was in Kathmandu, eventually finding it in the grounds of the University. Some three or four miles from my hotel, I found the only grass cricket pitch in the city, if not in the whole of Nepal. The facilities were very basic, but the welcome was the usual in this great city, greeted with much enthusiasm by one and all. The three days I visited them were the most memorable, getting to know them all, including a team of under-seventeens from Bombay (Mumbai), who were on a tour to play the Nepalese national team.

Nepal won the match, and I was told in no uncertain manner, to join them in the team photo. This I did after presenting a Creigiau cricket shirt to the man of the match, finding the whole event reported in the English language paper the next day. I would not have known this, if it had not been for a visit by the father of the recipient of the man-of-the-match award, to my hotel the next day.

There was to be a friendly match that day, and I was invited to play, again being greeted like a long lost son, being asked to bowl at the gathering players on the outfield. They seemed surprised that someone so old still played, with a stream of eager cricketers ready to chat at every turn. The interest in someone as ordinary as me was a little unnerving, but on reflection, I suppose not too many people go to Kathmandu and watch cricket.

As the start time approached, I began to realise that there were so many players ready to play, that I would be taking a game from one of them if I played, so decided to offer to Umpire instead. Apparently the cost of a match at this ground is astronomical in their terms, playing only a handful of games in a season at best.

The game was a very gentlemanly affair, with the tutors somewhat outplayed by the students, with luckily no difficult or controversial decisions for me as the umpire. During tea, I was again surrounded by one and all, inquiring of my involvement in the game back home, showing a considerable knowledge of the game, but most of all displaying an intense respect, especially for their elders, something not always present in Western society.

I spent some time wandering the area around the ground, as it was a particularly green area, with few people, and interesting walks. One walk became quite fascinating, when I came across a makeshift tent in the shape of a teepee. It was alongside a cultivated small field, where some sort of vegetables had grown, placed very close to the cricket ground. A group of six or seven young boys approached, ages ranging from four to twelve approximately. They were curious about my interest in the cricket, and of where I came from and why. Their English was limited, but the older boy explained that he looked after the group, and they lived in the make-shift tent, working the small plot of land. As far as I could tell, they were orphans, fending for themselves, but that is more of an assumption than a fact.

They were polite and in no way looking for a free meal or hand-outs, so I asked if they would be offended if I gave them some money to buy fruit or veg. etc. They humbly accepted the small gift, something I would never have thought to do back home, as it would be totally misinterpreted. I continued my walk, contemplating the sadness of their situation, getting my usual tearful reaction to the events, when I was aware of the group chasing after me calling my name. They had learned my nickname, Deadly, it being somewhat surreal to be called that in these surroundings. I turned, still somewhat tearful, to find the whole group of smiling faces waiting to give me a silver 20 rupee coin, in return for my gift to them.

I do not think I have to tell you the effect it had on me, but the same emotion envelopes me every time I recall the incident, even as I write this section. A lasting image remains, of the older boy, looking up at a passing jet, and asking, what is it like to be inside such a plane? I wonder if he has discovered that feeling yet.

After this episode, I decided to walk back to town, passing many well fed cows, along with grossly overcrowded vehicles, including the regulation three-wheeler converted Vespa Van, carrying as many as fifteen passengers, perched in some impossible looking positions, although the speed they travelled at posed little danger, even if they fell off. This everyday precarious mode of transport, seemed to offer no fears to young and old, with again the incredible calm of the people, shining like a beacon through their difficult way of life.

The following day was to be a day of indulgence for me, having booked a flight to see Mount Everest on the aptly named 'Buddha Air' airline. Before this, I wanted to visit the temples where the cremations took place, a very holy area on the river-bank. The architecture was awesome, the sights fascinating, with holy men covered in ash from the departed, proceeding with their chosen way, adding a sense of the unreal to our Western eyes. The images of this wondrous scene will stay with me far longer than the snapshots I took at the time. I recall an atmosphere of celebration of lives moved on, with the physical tasks, a mere by-product of dying. To describe the day-to-day workings of this extraordinary place, I feel would be superfluous, as the first impression of shock, soon dissipates into sheer admiration. It is almost as though sadness is drawn from the mourners, replaced by positive acceptance to the new day.

All around the temples, dotted around the hills surrounding the site, were many souvenir sellers, displaying jewellery and trinkets, as well as the musical drums, bells and in particular, the singing bowls, that for some reason stick in the memory. The sadness that overcame me at the outset was soon replaced by a feeling of calm, to say nothing of the revelation that death is merely a consequence of living, accepted by these lovely people with a dignity we could all learn from.

Dawn the following day entered my senses, with a explosion of anticipation. All the excitement of early adventures rushing through the mind, anticipating this new experience with an eagerness usually reserved for the excitement of that first kiss. The day did not disappoint, the weather was the best it had been for weeks, turning out to be the only morning where there was to be perfect visibility over the great Himalayas.

Arriving at the small airport shortly after dawn, walking past the obligatory gun-post, I settled down to wait for the flight to be called. There were no loud-speakers, although I was not aware of this, until one of the gate attendants frantically waved and called my name, in the hope of finding the missing passenger, me. His accent made my name unidentifiable, but I eventually was ushered to the small jet waiting close by. Buddha Air was proudly displayed on this seemingly brand-new plane, shining in the early morning sunshine, somewhat out of place amidst these basic surroundings.

We were soon winging our way on the easy route to the summit of Everest, the cost to me, hopefully aiding the economy of the region, although I felt guilty at being so privileged as to be able to take this flight.

The duration of the flight is incalculable to me now, but the emotion this trip evoked sends shivers down my spine. As we flew at around thirty thousand feet East, then swung left to follow the line of the Himalayas West, we were kept informed by the captain of the views at any particular point – until we flew, seemingly adjacent to Everest itself. I simply cannot find words to describe the view itself, as I am sure we have all witnessed different sights during our lives that defy description. This was one such case for me, the photographs I took through the plane's windows, can never do justice to the scene. The next thing said by the captain had a similar effect on my mind. He said, "If you look beyond Everest, you will see Tibet. That was it for me, the flood gates opened in a surge of emotion greater than any I had previously experienced, I wept with uncontrolled intensity until we eventually returned to Kathmandu.

I simply can't explain why this occurred, and will not even attempt to do so, but the feelings towards Tibet and her people, had taken on a new significance that is undiminished. Would that I could pour some of these feelings into one or two politicians, at least giving them the opportunity to see a little more clearly the pure joy of being, without all the trappings of prejudice.

I am sure that my fellow passengers that day, would have imagined all sorts of scenarios about my reactions, probably thinking I was in pain, not realising it was quite the opposite, and as it is very unlikely any of those German tourists will ever see this record of the events, it will never be explained or understood.

Back in the town, I had chatted to a number of locals from the hotel, some of whom had escaped from Tibet, although they were a little reluctant to talk too much of their experiences. They were however, so helpful in directing me to the interesting sites to see around the town, one in particular who had aspirations to travel, practised his English on me as often as possible. It was clear to me that he was in a Catch-22 situation, being an immigrant in Nepal with limited access to work. As a student, he obviously had a struggle to feed and cloth himself, and was very quick to accept an offer from me to take some of my clothes when I left, giving me more room in my case for the trinkets I had acquired during my stay.

Before leaving, I really wanted to take a walk up into the foothills of the Himalayas, so I acquired the services of a guide to assist me in the venture. Again my poor memory for names is evident, as the guide's name eludes me, but his calm demeanour from start to finish was exemplary, dealing with car problems easily, along with constant encouragement to me in my struggle to keep up with him.

We had agreed to a four hour walk, taking us over a succession of ridges, hopefully ending at a very old Temple perched on top of a hill. The effort was well worth it, for it was like walking back into another century, with craftsmen and women living in this remote village within the temple grounds. There were Hindu and Buddhist Icons for sale, although it seems unlikely to me that there would be many takers, as they were so far from the tourist trails.

The whole day was a satisfying conclusion to the journey to this mesmerising land, and the journey itself had laid to rest a yearning I had, to possibly spend a lot more time here. It had quickly become apparent that I would never have come to terms with the harsh realities of everyday life, let alone the limited food choices.

With a sense of relief, I returned home, bulging with more treas-ured experiences from the sights and sounds of this Himalayan Wonderland, sad that my mind had to leave, but peacefully accepting the reality. In quiet moments the images return to pacify the rigours of daily life: the prayer wheels still spinning outside the Buddhist Temple in Kathmandu; the gentle faces of the Buddhist Monks, blissfully gliding through the grounds, spreading a calm that seemed even to hypnotise the huge families of apes that lived in the temple; the youngsters living in the grounds of the University cricket ground, shadowing the elite band of cricketers, vibrantly pursuing their sport in their oasis in the hills; children, with their treasured toy, a hoop with a stick, oblivious of the 21st. Century, strengthening their bodies and minds for their particular path through life. So much to savour in this short excursion. I marvel at my good fortune.

Ponty & Further India Trips

The need to earn a living took over again, although I must confess it is more like pleasure to me than work, trying always to give value for money without the flamboyance of some in my trade. I have always taken a keen interest in the local scene, with my involvement in Local Government, and a strong desire to see progress in the town's infrastructure. The Old Bridge in particular, has always prompted ideas for improvement in me, for I cannot see how a road bridge can remain adjacent to this amazing piece of architecture, blocking its features from the passer by.

The shopping area of the town still covers the same acreage, yet there is only half the occupation of the premises, leaving ample opportunities for the town area to be developed, yet one after the other, the schemes come and go, leaving a sad mix of old and older buildings decorating a unique, but unattractive landscape. Not least in these observations, is the chronic traffic situation that seems to blight all towns, creating in Ponty, a particularly difficult traffic flow situation. There is a restriction on traffic turning right into Taff Street, the main shopping area and car parking entrance. At these lights, only buses and taxis are permitted to turn right, a restriction that has been a bone of contention since it was introduced a few years ago.

Every six months or so, a couple of policemen would take up positions in Taff Street, stopping and booking any motorist turning right. It had become the normal procedure over the months, to ignore the signs, as the alternative was to find another way of turning, or driving to a roundabout further on, then returning from the other direction so as to turn left, adding to the road congestion, to say nothing of the frustration it caused.

One day, a friend of mine was passing near to my shop, complaining that "they were at it again," stopping and booking motorists in Taff Street. I was going that way, and viewed the situation, getting involved by asking the officers why they were enforcing a rule that was frequently overlooked by their own colleagues, when driving through that set of lights, to say nothing of the danger caused by the hesitations and detours that the restriction caused drivers to take.

I was put in my place by the one officer, who was obviously having a bad day. He advised me to complain to the station some few yards away, so I did so without much success. I decided to take direct action, positioning myself at the lights, I strongly advised drivers to obey the rule and NOT turn right, which they all did. The consequence of my action was that the regular flow of cars turning into the clutches of the Law stopped.

The particular officer's day was getting worse, and it was he who summoned me across the road to discuss the situation. That meant me jay-walking across a busy road to stand roadside of railings to talk to him. I declined the request suggesting using the Zebra crossing for safety reasons. We eventually met, where he and a woman constable confronted me, threatening to arrest me if I stopped any more motorists turning right, to which I suggested that I was doing my duty as a citizen, stopping people breaking the law.

It was a close call as I considered if it would be worth the trouble to take that step and get arrested. As I was in the middle of a day's work, I opted not to do so, but had I done so it would at least have been another experience to look back on. An interesting end to this episode, is that the officer left the woman PC to keep an eye on my activities, so when I positioned myself facing the traffic at the said junction, I realised that traffic approaching the turn could see the Police uniform, and refrained from turning without my doing anything.

There were no more bookings that day, and after one further episode with the same officer, the matter was resolved with a letter from a senior officer stating that no police vehicles would be allowed to turn right at that junction, except in an emergency. It confirmed what had been common knowledge, and there has been a singular lack of activity in this field ever since.

Meeting 16th July 2007. Derick and Margaret have given me a whole new perspective on one particular era, and even more about dates, even with a letter I had sent him from the boat while crossing The Bay of Biscay. This includes a plan for a purpose built darkroom, and details of my trip home from India, some of which had been lost to my memory completely. The letter lists the cities I had just left, and the itinerary for the next part of the journey.

More than this, Margaret had revealed information about some of my thinking around the January and February of 1963. This clarifies some of the dates of some of the stories in this book. The date of my trip to India is now confirmed as September 1962 to January 4th. 1963. Most of the adventures took place before these dates, and some adjustments should now be made, however, on reflection, I don't see a benefit in such actions, so it remains as-is.

Even more important revelations are about my approach to the fairer sex. Margaret was in a class in the girls' school in Treforest that contained some of the girls that I had been so interested in. Luckily, her memory is much better than mine, and she remembers some details that are a revelation to me, or rather, an embarrassment. It appears that when I met a girl at a dance, I would tell them that my dad had an oil well, and would then listen to their reply to make sure they had their brains switched on enough, to warrant an interest by me. I have a zero recollection of this, but, embarrassingly, I must admit that it says something about my mindset at the time. I trust Margaret's recollections of these periods completely, even though the facts do not exactly paint me in a very good light.

The references to some of the names did make the heart-strings twang a little, as my mind has a distinct picture of some of them. Novelo in particular and her mum had been good friends, and, it seems, Pat had been in that same class.

I am now sitting at the computer at 4.30am, the morning after the revelations from Margaret and Derick, having slept little with all the new information planted in the brain. My next task is to decide whether I should put the information as a separate item, or try to insert the relevant facts into their position in the book. For now, I think some sleep is necessary for the busy day ahead.

My work as a photographer entered the digital age at last. The timing of this move was about right on reflection, as equipment had dipped to a more reasonable price, and the advances in the technology had stabilised to a great degree. I shall not dwell long on the pros and cons of this system over traditional film, but suffice to say that I, and many of my colleagues in the trade, still use film for wedding photography, the quality being different as opposed to better.

The advantages of the new system are obvious for all to see, however I have seen a huge shift in attitudes of many new photographers, in that they seem to take many shots of each pose, in the hope that one will be satisfactory. Personally I do not subscribe to this method, preferring to get the subject as I want it, take the one shot, then confidently move on to the next. I have also come to the conclusion that best results are obtained working in manual mode, trusting in my judgment of the light as opposed to the camera's.

There was to be another trip to India, this time to a friend's wedding. Girish to Vidula. I needed no excuse to re-visit that great sub-continent, and it was not long before I was gliding over the vast corrugated roofs of the dwellings on the approach to Mumbai (Bombay) Airport, to land again in that city I had left by sea all those years ago.

Girish had been a member of our cricket team in Creigiau for a number of years while he worked locally, along with another fellow Indian, Sameep, who, in a year or so would follow Girish's example, and return to India to marry. Mumbai seemed to me no different after all these years, with the humidity levels as oppressive as ever. The trip was less for nostalgia, more a chance to savour the culture of this mysterious place on a personal note, knowing the people I was visiting.

I was greeted at the airport by Girish's sister and his cousin. He was holding a placard at the exit to greet me to Mumbai. It boldly stated, "DEADLY", accompanied by a drawing of three cricket stumps being broken by a cricket ball. It did the trick and I was soon chatting to Girish's relatives as though I had known them for years, tasting the pleasure of being driven along the unchanged streets of the capital to meet mum at their home. What a delightful lady she is, making me so welcome in their home. The smile on my face was fixed, as I met up with friends in this old haunt, this time it was a reunion, along with a unique opportunity to see something of their customs, meet his bride for the first time and forge a friendship with both families. Girish had even arranged for a meeting with another ex-Creigiau cricketer, Veejay who now lived in Mumbai with his new wife.

The wedding was a brief glimpse into one aspect of their ways, allowing me the privilege of witnessing it at first hand. The unfortunate side of the visit was the searing heat and humidity that drained me physically, causing me to leave earlier than I would have wished. Vidula was now another friend from this continent, to be joined a year later by their lovely daughter Chetra. I still enjoy the occasional visit to their home near London, where I have had the pleasure of meeting their families again.

Cricket was still the main feature of the summers at home, where the friendships forged over the years at the club strengthened with each successive season. I spent many a lazy Saturday evening at the local Indian Restaurant, sharing cricket chat from the days proceedings. Jonathan and I were firm friends at the club, sharing a similar mindset to the game we both played, to say nothing of our taste in food.

He was one of two captains I played under who rated the top in my book. He, along with Tony Hallet, epitomised the spirit of the game, always giving total respect to all on the field of play. If Jonathan had been in better health, I am sure he would have gone on to even more successes on the cricket field, adding to his achievements that far. The major surgery he had undergone some years earlier had given him a new lease of life, used to its full, he was, and still is, an inspiration to many, especially me.

Often I see stories of great heroics with triumphs over adversity, usually by stars of stage or sport, yet the unsung fortitude of people like Jonathan are equally as deserving of attention, so I, in my small way, pay tribute here to a friend who shines like a beacon amidst the galaxies of this astonishing human race.

Soon it was to be Sameep's turn to tie the knot, although he spent much of his free time preparing wickets for the club, playing and joining us at the Spice Indian Restaurant in Pontyclun. I will start with the wicket preparation, which included brushing, scarifying and cutting the pitches, followed by rolling. Sameep would volunteer for any of these tasks enthusiastically, however his attempts one day caused more than a chuckle. Dave Price, Arthur Cook, Jonathan and myself delegated the square cut to Sameep. This entailed parallel cuts to and fro, to leave a regular pattern over the whole square.

The end product was more like the tracks of a swarm of panicking snakes, much to the amusement of all, including Sameep, who was occasionally reminded of the event at our weekly after-match gettogethers. On the field he was somewhat intense, chastising himself for any minor mishap on his part, adding to the overall pleasure of this amazing game.

His prowess with bat and ball was not to be underestimated, for he contributed much to the club in the few years he played for us. His admiration of others in the club made him a good team man. In particular, he often waxed lyrical about a certain Martin Powell, a batsman who would hit the ball further than seemed possible.

One aspect of his time with us had nothing to do with cricket, but the journey we made from his digs in Taffs Well to the ground in Creigiau. We had to drive through an avenue of trees up a hill to

Pentyrch, the trees forming a tunnel of green that was magical, especially to Sameep. His silence during the mile climb only broken with an occasional whisper of, "It's so green". I hope we all value the simple pleasures of such sights fully.

Sameep soon left us to return to his home in India, shortly followed by an announcement of his forthcoming marriage, along with invitations to Jonathan and myself, as well as some of his workmates at GE's plant in Nantgarw. This was not to be missed, so plans were soon in place to attend the wedding of Sameep to Neeru.

Jonathan's dad had agreed to transport us to Heathrow, and apart from a considerable delay on the M4, we made our flight, eager to taste the wonders of the new adventure. Since the trip, I have pondered on what it would have been like to have Jonathan with me on my early trips, with his sense of humour, his fortitude and his stubborn resolve. My instinct tells me that he would have shared all my adventures, reinforced by many of his own. This trip would prove to be a confirmation of two kindred spirits sharing perceptions of the great sub-continent.

From beginning to end, we were on the same wavelength, respecting the Hindu ways, sharing in the traditions of this land, soaking in the very breath of the Indian Nation, smiling and crying with the sights and sounds we were witnessing. I have made scores of friends in my life, few have touched my soul like Jonathan.

This trip had all the hallmarks of a classic, sudden decision, followed by a swift departure, leaving no time for second thoughts or doubts. From the moment we were met by Krishna Rao at the airport in Delhi, we felt at home, driven to our hotel through familiar traffic to me, but an instant baptism for Jonathan in the fantasy world of road ethics in this part of the world. Krishna had been asked by Sameep to look after us both, transport us to any places of interest, generally making sure we did not get into too much mischief.

We soon found our feet, strolling the local area soaking up the atmosphere. Although it was quite familiar to me, it was all new to Jonathan, yet he seemed to accept instantly the simplistic complexity of this mostly Hindu society. I recall his almost permanent smile as we savoured the sights, sounds and smells of this unique part of the world. One of the first encounters with the locals was at a small Hindu shrine very close to our hotel, we approached, to be greeted with the customary "Namaste" and a prayer gesture with clasped hands, returned by myself, quickly followed by Jonathan. He embraced the customs without question, something that had taken a long time for myself years earlier.

We returned several times to this shrine, although not understanding much of the intricacies of the religion, to make small donations to their Gods with offerings of the traditional flowers, receiving the blessing from the Holy Man with the traditional red Tilak to the forehead. All these actions seemed to fortify us both, despite my strong views regarding religions generally. We never discussed that subject specifically, but I suspect we were both on a similar wavelength.

That evening we were taken by our man Krishna to eat in the centre of Delhi, to be faced with a large circular shopping area, the architecture of which reminded me of Rome or Athens. The uniformity of the buildings made it difficult to ascertain where you were, making the job of finding your car after a walk somewhat confusing. Even more bizarre was the restaurant we were taken to, Burger King, K.F.C. or Pizza Express we were told were the safe options, so for now we took his advice, joining a crowd that could have been anywhere in a city in the UK in Burger King.

It was explained that the following day we would start early to make Sameep's wedding day in plenty of time. We were told it would be about a three-hour journey, the wedding started around 3.00pm. so we agreed to be ready to travel around 8.00am. By 10.00am we were a little worried, but having some knowledge of many Indians' concept of time, we were not unduly worried, and we eventually got under way with what we thought was plenty of time to reach our destination.

By this stage we were both looking forward to seeing Sameep and his new bride, becoming increasingly concerned when the three hours turned into four, then five and beyond. There seemed no urgency with Krishna or his driver, who insisted all was well, and that the wedding went on a long time, with no chance of missing anything. We eventually arrived some two hours after the scheduled start, were taken to the Swagat Hotel and advised to have a rest for an hour or so, then they would return to take us to the celebrations.

Jonathan and I looked at each other, and with one voice said No, we will go straight there. Splashing our faces with some cold water, we quickly changed and were on our way to the wedding. We had of course not understood the way their celebrations go, but it was just as well we arrived when we did, as we would not have seen Sameep for some time if we had delayed.

We arrived just before he changed into his wedding attire, having a chance to chat and circulate amongst the many guests already assembled. This was a grand affair with food and dance in evidence everywhere, the customary lack of importance of TIME obvious, so we both took the opportunity to savour the delights of some food, along with a very active dance session around the resident drumming duo, much to the delight of many guests. If my memory serves me right, I used some moves reminiscent of John Travolta in one of his films, much to the delight of some of the guests. Unfortunately my stamina was not what it used to be, so an early retirement from the scene ended a promising career in Bollywood.

I do not intend to give a detailed description of the wedding ceremony, however, the protracted nature of the hours of ceremony, mixed with photo sessions, then more ceremony, gave Jonathan and me time to talk to the families and friends milling around. While Jonathan chatted, I took more photos in between dancing with the exuberant guests, one or two of which had definitely had a tipple or two.

One dominant image of the proceedings was that of the flies surrounding the floodlighting illuminating the whole area. The good thing about that was, that they did not seem bother us too much. The eight-piece brass band heralded the arrival of the now resplendent bridegroom, along with the magnificent white horse that was to take the groom on a tour around the village. He was followed by many of the guests, although we remained at the venue as the swarms of flies followed the well lit procession.

I was surprised at the informal nature of the ceremony, but not at the prolonged time scale, the groom taking centre stage well into the evening. Neeru eventually arrived, resplendent in her red attire, dreamily gliding amongst frantic dancers to join her intended on the raised area at one end of the hall. Her serious demeanour must be the norm, and here I must say there was an air of calm and respect pervading the whole event.

During these protracted ceremonies Jonathan and I chatted amongst relatives, although Jonathan was quite the centre of attraction with his almost permanent smile mesmerising the ladies, who seemed captivated by his striking eye colour. I was content to sit back, soaking in the seemingly endless celebrations, and we were privileged to be invited to the couple on the stage area to be photographed with Neeru and Sameep. By this stage I had taken a few snaps myself, feeling obliged to try to get Neeru to smile, something she seemed reluctant to do. Finally, I managed, although I am still not sure it was the right way to go at such times.

With all the chat between us all, the only person we did not get to talk to was Neeru, for by the time things became more informal, Jonathan and I were so tired, that we made our exit, leaving the still large crowd eating and chatting. We returned to what must have been the only hotel in the small village, to face the room we had only briefly seen on arrival. We spent that night telling jokes and generally savouring the days events, while trying not to notice the dead cockroaches and flies that seemed to be everywhere.

We had slept, or not, fully clothed including caps, (the cricket variety), yet it was all so normal that somehow it did not matter. Next morning, we were collected by our intrepid driver and Krishna, to be returned to Delhi, hopefully a little quicker than our outward journey. No way, our sleepy heads were taken along roads, that our instincts told us were way off track, so when we arrived at the banks of the Ganges, we realised it was a diversion for our travel companions to briefly bath in 'Mother Ganga', and why not?

The whole journey back from Muzaffarnagar took seven hours, yet looking back, it had to be, or we would not have soaked in the heartbeat of this extraordinary country, leaving us both hugely admiring the Karma of this Nation.

Back at the White House Hotel in Delhi we caught up on the sleep we had been denied the last day or two, enjoying the luxury of the air-conditioned rooms. All this luxury was such a contrast from my travels as a youth, although I have to admit that it would have been a struggle to have lived the way I had then.

Lots more to see, so with the continued help of Krishna along with his driver, who had been put at our disposal by Sameep for the few days remaining of our stay, we did the touristy things, in particular to the Taj Mahal and the Red Fort. I was to save the one requested visit for the last day, to try to locate the ruins I used to walk through on my walks in Delhi some 46 years earlier.

First though, it was to be The Red Fort. Majestic and massive, yet of little interest to us for reasons I can not explain, so we were soon on our way to the Taj Mahal. The last time I had caught a glimpse of this structure, was from a train on my way to Bombay in early November of 1962, still too weak from the last attack of dysentery, so all I got was a fleeting glimpse through the train's window as we steamed by. This was a chance to really view the structure up close and personal, so we took our place behind the long queue, to be told by one of the attendants, to go to the front of the queue, explaining that foreign visitors had priority. I stubbornly insisted on waiting with the locals, much to Krishna's annoyance. In the meantime, Jonathan was approached by a local wanting to practice his English, and as they chatted Jonathan realised that there was a metal detector to be entered before access to the Taj Mahal would be permitted, and due to his pacemaker, he was ushered through to sit in the shade until I got through.

This was just as well, as Jonathan had not been at all well that day, and it gave him a chance to rest a while. I eventually made it through, and we made our way past a host of souvenir stalls eager to sell trinkets of all descriptions. We left the bargaining to Krishna, who acquired a selection of rings, necklaces and bangles for the folks back home. Then, like the opening sequence to a Hollywood film, (or should I say Bollywood) we passed through a surrounding building's doorway to the sight of that great monument, gleaming in the seemingly permanent sunshine.

No words I can find would adequately describing the splendour of this marble masterpiece, so I leave it to every individual to draw their own pictures in their minds. We both simply stood, soaking in the scene, then strolled along the walkways beside the pools, but not approaching too close to the main building. For my part, I did not want to join the considerable crowds jockeying for places to take their souvenir photos within the building itself, preferring to take a seat in a quiet sidewalk and meditate a while, watching the chipmunks playing in the grounds.

All was well with the world as we left to take the short walk to the car park, where our transport waited. But before we took a couple of steps, we were implored by an enterprising young boy to allow him to convey us to our destination on his three wheel bike-taxi. We paused, looked at each other, and climbed aboard, hanging on for our lives as the exuberant rider showed us how fast he could make that three-wheeler go. The lad's zest for life was infectious, and his endeavours will, I am sure, ensure him a considerable success in his life.

Some last minute purchases through the car window saw us on the road back to Delhi, with me contemplating the chances of finding that elusive sight of my regular walks all those years earlier, through the ruins of the old temples. My recollections of the site were very clear in my mind, but the name of the place I was not so sure of. The name, Qutb Minar was the only one I had thought it might be, so Sameep had arranged for us to be taken there.

Next day we drove to the site. Regrettably, as soon as we stopped in the car park, I knew it was not the place. The site was a renovation of an old site, sanitised and arranged into a safe tourist attraction. I went off on my own, walking in the directions I remembered, yet nothing struck a chord. I even tried to locate the hostel which had been close by, with the Buddhist enclave adjacent, but it was not to be. I still long to find that place that had made such an impression on me, and in quiet moments, I still hear the joyous laughter of the children dropping into the pool in the middle of that old temple, as

I made my way into the centre of Delhi.

On reflection, it would be too simple if all the questions were answered, giving something still to be solved another day. Rather like the meeting with the ladies in Dover on the way home from my first visit to India, it remains an intriguing mystery for me to wrestle with.

Time to return home with a bag full of new memories, having travelled for the first time with a friend, making this trip that little bit different to my usual. Sameep had been a wonderful host, the memories of the events will last long in the conscious pattern of experiences this life has offered me so far. The mass of jigsaw pieces, making up an existence on this earth, combining to create a massive picture in the mind of each individual; each different and unique, ready to be interwoven with our fellow man, hopefully creating a climate for a more trusting world order.

Humility, tolerance, and respect must come from within each individual, as this can be sustained and grow, whereas an imposed regime such as politics or religion, would have to be ratified by that mind before acceptance. Therefore history, which is notoriously subject to change through time, should be used only as a guide to the historic happenings.

Recent Events & Revisits

April 2009 was to be the final curtain for Jonathan. He died aged 30, less than half-way through the average life-span, yet leaving mountains of memories for all who knew him. His last year of life was shared with Jenny, his partner, giving Jonathan such well-deserved happiness through that final stage. A few weeks before he died, they learned that she was pregnant. Jenny gave birth to their son, Dylan Jon, in December.

Such events, so sad, yet poignant, gave rise to positive thoughts to so many of those who went through the events of those weeks, prompting responses from myself in a renewed vigour to carry on some of the work he had started. I am sure it was part of my decision to take a break from the Summer proceedings, and plan a short trip to gather extra information for this book.

This trip was arranged for Saturday 13th June, leaving Cardiff at 2.00pm, but, as usual, the cricket team was a man short, and being a little bit fanatical about my sport, and ignoring the knowledge of the pain to follow such activity, I agreed and switched my ticket to 9.30am Sunday from Cardiff. It proved to be a good decision, as the match was most memorable. For those who do not play cricket, the exhilaration of an unexpected win will have little impact, but to those initiated into the finer points of the game, it was a rush of some magnitude. The details are really not important, but the fact that every player contributed to the success, meant that the final edge for four, was just the icing on the cake. Puppy, that was even better than my edges! (Phil Bartle and other cricket friends will know what I mean.)

Sunday morning arrived with me in a rather sleepy state, but the exertions of the previous day were all forgotten, and I arrived at the bus station in Pontypridd in fine mood. The X4 was just disappearing out of the station, leaving three minutes early. Good start this, I thought, but two minutes later another bus arrives. This one had broken down much earlier, and was trying to make up time. We sped to Cardiff and arrived in good time for my connection to London.

The 8.30 had still not left, so I was ushered aboard an hour earlier than expected. As I traversed the aisle, my daughter and two friends on a day out to London, greeted me with "Dad" from the back of the bus. It was quite by chance that we had ended up on the same bus, but for their sakes, it was good that our destinations were quite different. Things were going well for me, and how nice to have a little company with Katy to the big city. On arrival they made off for their batch of London goodies, and I moved on to my train to Croydon, and another visit to some young old friends.

Girish and Vidula and their daughter Chetra, along with Girish's mum had always given me a warm welcome whenever I had visited them, both in the UK or in India, and I was invited to stay over before moving on to my next destination, Leysdown. Next day, Girish and I left together for Victoria station, where I went off to my connection, and Girish to work.

This trip had been a sudden, and late decision, prompted by a stressful week or two, and a desire to get some more information on some of my early travelling for this book. Since starting writing, I felt a big change in my attitude to many things, in particular memories that had lain dormant for years, were reappearing at a frightening rate of knots. I felt as if I were being overwhelmed with the weight of thoughts surging in my mind, and even my attendance at my usual jazz gigs could not stop the mind wandering.

Meditate and chill out, that was foremost in my mind now, with no specific plan of travel, and no pre-conceived idea of the outcome. I thought back to attitudes I had taken in earlier years, when generally I had made plans, and had become quite annoyed if they did not come to fruition. I was determined to smile at whatever came before me on this trip. It would be a matter of "c'est la vie", and go with the flow.

After 36 hours of the trip, I felt liberated, clearly seeing a path I wanted to take, moving smoothly from one task to another. First, it was to be the place where I had first ventured into self-employment.

Leysdown-on-sea, on the Isle of Sheppey, Kent. It had been 50 years since I arrived with Barry to try our luck in business. The possibility of finding any of the old places was remote, but just being there may prompt a memory or two. Train and bus eventually got me to my destination, and to my great delight, I stepped off the bus to be facing The Barn, next to the Rose and Crown pub, where we had first set up a temporary dark room. It had also been the location of the encounter with the electric storm. I subsequently discovered from the present landlord, that it is a listed building, that being the reason for its survival.

It was now a Tattoo business, but was closed that day, denying me the opportunity of a look inside, however the landlord Dave Smith, assured me the old steep ladder to the upper room was still there. Great memories, and a good start to my day. I took a couple of photos for the archive, and wandered down the main street to see if the campsite was still in operation. It sure was; same name, and still a caravan campsite, but with luxury caravans in place of the very basic ones that I remembered.

At every corner I would meet another local with more and more details of the old place. It seemed that little had changed, including the basic layout of the place. Central Beach Caravan Park is still in operation on the same plot, and it took no time to locate the spot where our old caravan had stood. More pictures and a visit to the new site club where I had so many memories. The then boss Mr. Frank Purvis had made way for another owner, who had only recently passed on. At this same visit I spoke to a lady who turned out to be a relative of Mr. Purvis.

Two out of two so far, but could it continue? Indeed it could. The incident with the busking and the subsequent fish supper, had to be investigated, and sure enough still there, still a fish and chip shop, and still bearing the old name as well as the new owners name: GREENO'S FISH BAR had satisfied the taste buds all those years ago, and it was so satisfying to see it still trading.

While investigating these old haunts, the clouds began to roll in, and a storm was imminent. It is ironic that the ensuing thunderstorm occurred at around the same time as the incident 50 years earlier. As the streaks of lightning and the roars of thunder came closer, the landlord and some friends chatted on outside the Rose and Crown, enjoying an ice cream from the vendor on the street. He turned out to be a stall holder that used to visit my home town of Pontypridd, small world. No fireball this time, but it gave the moment an extra zip.

As the last bus back to Sheerness was 6.30pm, I decided to stay the night, and soon managed to find accommodation in a chalet, but not before enquiring with locals about getting to the location of my main darkroom, set up in April of 1959. All I could remember was that it was a shed behind a council house, around two to three miles away, and I used my motorcycle to go back and forth. Easily solved, there were only six such houses on the road in to Leysdown, and they would be easy to locate. Taxis were another matter, there were

none in Leysdown. Luckily, the guy who had given me this information said he would be delighted to take me there if I could wait a
while for him to take his very pregnant wife on some urgent call. And
so he did, taking me to within 50 yards of the said council houses.

The surrounding buildings made it all so different, but as I
approached I got a distinct feeling that it was the third house in, that
was the most likely. I approached the side entrance and rang the
bell, a lady answered and I tried to explain my story, we were joined
by her husband, and they explained that they were the oldest residents of the block, and they had only been there fifteen years. My
heart sank a little but I explained I had been in a shed behind one
of the houses, and I thought it was theirs. They agreed to let me have
a look at the rear of their house, but asked me to wait while they
took down a board above the gate to then open the wooden garden
gate. As it opened my eyes could hardly believe my eyes. There was
the shed, 50 years older, but definitely where all those years ago, I
had set up a darkroom, and where I spent so much time developing
and printing. How small it seemed now with the tools and work-
bench, with no sign of a blacked out window. The red painted door
on its third or forth coat since I had entered and locked myself in
for the night's work.

Another success, and after the obligatory photo, I thanked the
couple, and returned to the car where my driver was almost as
pleased as I had been. Perhaps I will return and check out the new
arrival one day, but in the meantime, I trust all went well.

I went to the owner of the chalet's restaurant for a meal that
evening, having had a nostalgic wander around the village, making a
quick visit to the club for an orange juice. For me, having an early
night was usually a shocking waste of precious time, but on this occasion it proved a good idea.

I awoke to a rustling sound, to discover rabbits playing under and
around the chalet, and not having any desire to sleep on, I decided
to make an early start. I returned the key through the door of the
owner's restaurant, said farewell to the rabbits, and caught the first
bus back to Sheerness. I had deliberately made no set plans for the
trip, and so I drifted to the next moment, and allowed my feet take
me to the next move.

I stood at the booking desk at the rail station, and inquired the
price of a ticket to Dover. The price was right and the train was
waiting, so off I went. Dover seemed a world away from my memory
of it, and when the bus dropped me at the Ferry Terminal, and I was
informed there was a ferry leaving imminently, I joined the few foot

passengers and we were whisked onto a bus to do the run-around to the waiting ferry. All this was so different from my early encounters with Ferry travel.

First it was passport control, with everyone off the bus and then back on. Then to the X-Ray dept., all off the bus again, through the security check and into a holding room. A toilet visit seemed a good idea, as I really did not know when I would get another chance. I exit the toilet, and, no one in sight, they had gone without me. Not to worry, as one of the security ladies smiled and took complete control. Into an official car and I was taken to the embarkation point and got a lift with a group of American tourists on a luxury coach.

On board this luxurious ferry I faced an exuberant mass of excited school children, furiously flirting with each other, and charging around the vessel chasing their own tails. All this seemed to exude the same excitement I had felt on my early trips to and from the Continent. I sat in silence and soaked in the atmosphere, with a smile on my face of inward pleasure. As if by magic, all the throng disappeared as we approached Calais, when they rejoined their vehicles, and just a handful of us foot passengers gathered at the disembarking point. Maybe my silent smiles had been noticed, as while we waited, I was approached by a member of the cloth, who approached me to try and convince me of the need to be saved. I assured him that I knew where the life jackets were kept, and I was confident of our ability to get to dry land safely. I then noticed he was with a group of twenty or so very beautiful young ladies, and my thoughts raced to a conclusion of "If I were in your place, I would not be chatting to some stranger".

Enough of such diversions, I set foot on French soil for the first time in many a long year, and set off to walk to town. This was the new part of this trip, as I had never stayed in Calais, but simply passed through. I eventually found the tourist information office, and got directions to a small B&B in my price range, and decided to walk the beach route to my bed for the night.

Moments to take stock; and after a much needed rest, I ventured to a local bar to put down my thoughts so far. My travels in my youth were frantic and non-stop, without realising there are times when you must stand back and look at yourself, and where you are headed. Without these breaks from the action of life, it can be difficult to see what is right in front of you. This short trip had cleared my mind of a lot of question marks. What is sometimes most obvious, is most difficult to see. Again I had a pleasing feeling that I am more at peace with myself, no frantic desires to achieve a certain goal, or change the way other people see me. That really is not my concern as I am more and more convinced that we must know ourselves, and only then will we begin to know others, and be non-judgemental.

These thoughts seem to pour out in bursts, and at such times I always wonder if they can be of help or interest to others, but of course, that is not for me to speculate.

I now intended to return to Dover to attempt to locate the houses on the way out of the port, where forty nine years ago, I had that beautiful contact with some locals, while clearing snow from their driveways. It was not to be, after most of the day on foot and a taxi ride, I failed in this last endeavour of this trip.

All in all, I am very pleased at the outcome of this trip, and have to admit that it has re-kindled an urge to travel more.

Blast from the Past

Since moving into 3, Ceridwen Terrace to live and work, a strangely ordered existence had taken over my everyday life, giving me a freedom to explore the Self in a more orderly fashion. It was a liberation that seemed to open doors previously closed to me, the Buddhist Meditation being central to this, leading me away from my old perceptions, into new clearer visions of others in relation to myself. My acceptance of situations has been a major plus for me, eliminating much questioning of superfluous subjects, including a coming to terms with the onset of vertigo. The dramatic start of this curious condition in the waiting room of the local police station, still haunts a backwater of my brain's recordings, with the whirlpool sensation, (that has been experienced by so many), leaving my brain feeling like a bowl of jelly as one walks, creating a world around me that refuses to stay still. How many more people will accuse me of drinking too much, I wonder.

The telephone rang. It was a dreamy quiet Wednesday: some photographic inquiry, or maybe some cricket or table tennis info. No, it was an Indian gent inquiring if I was, "Derek Lewis, photographer, from Pontypridd who was in Bombay in 1962, at the YMCA hostel, on the final leg of a hitch-hike adventure". Somewhat bemused, I replied "yes". "Did you sport a bushy ginger beard". I replied yes, still somewhat disbelieving of what I was hearing.

"I've found you after all this time, I am Ron Andrews (not the typical Indian name), the guy you befriended in that hostel all those years ago". "Do you remember the wedding gift sent from India in 1964, there were two blankets, one brown and one green". "Yes, I do". I began to realise who this guy was, as I frantically searched the memory banks for information. "Are you the chap I offered a job to, in a letter, saying I would pay you £8.00 a week if you got to my photo printing business in Pontypridd". That was it, and although I had no recollection of meeting him in Bombay, all the other pieces of the jigsaw fell neatly into place.

It turned out that he had always retained the basic info. on me, and had eventually found me on the internet. It seems that the original letter was his passport to obtaining a visa to work away from India, ending up in Toronto, Canada, where he worked on Canadian Railways for many years. Now retired, he and his wife, Sheila were considering a journey to the UK to visit friends, hoping to meet up with me to renew a friendship started 47 years earlier.

Ever since this first contact from Canada, I have tried to find a picture of the original meeting, but it totally eludes me, even after he visited with Sheila, staying with me for a week in Pontypridd. The only glimmer of recognition came when we met for the first time, when a fleeting image flew through my mind, but immediately left again. Regardless of this, it was a most pleasant reunion, reliving the separate images we both retained from the past, and catching up on all that had occurred in the interim period.

I had arranged a dinner party for the day after their arrival, to introduce them to some of my present friends along with my family. They included jazz, cricket and personal friends, trying to show them a cross-section of the life I was now embroiled in. Even one of the blankets, (the green one) was on display for them to see, carefully stored all these years by Elaine. It had apparently been dispatched by Ron's sister from Bombay, as Ron was working in Kuwait at the time, this fact was a probable reason why we had not understood who had sent the gift.

Such a pleasant interlude, with names from the past reappearing, establishing a strong bond that I am sure will flourish, perhaps even through our respective children in years to come. I had never before realised the significance of, "parting is such sweet sorrow", yet a visit to Toronto is not out of the question for some future trip.

I reflect on the mountain of small, sometimes insignificant, sights, sounds or even feelings that invade the mind from the past, inexorably drifting, the old into new, sifting, sorting and evolving into a new being. I keep returning to the wooden bed I lay on for days in Delhi, soaking in the sight of those Buddhist Monks going about their daily tasks, in what seems to me a time-warp that still exists, if only in my mind. For how can any image exist anywhere but in one's own mind? Yet that scene has become a fixture in me, transported somehow without any obvious link, leaving me changed, yet the same 'Self'.

As I draw closer to the final stages of the story so far, I ponder on the people of my age, along with those from the past, that seem to have influenced my thinking in some way relative to this subject, a list that seems to grow every time the subject is broached by me. I shall mix up all these names (excluding blood-relatives), past and present, and will deliberately not specify why I include them, except to say all are for positive reasons. Dalai Lama, Garry Lineker, Sir Francis Chichester, Bob Pemberthy, Rob Smith, John Arlott, Rev Richards-Clarke, Sir Vivian Richards, Gandhi, The Lady Beggar in Delhi with one leg, Muralidarin, Yehudi Menuhin, Chris R, Suma R, Tony Hallet, Pat, E, Brett Lee, Robin, Donald Campbell, etc, etc…

I have concluded never to close the door on any subject or idea, facing frequent situations where it may be painful, but necessary to change my mind, as more information becomes available, trying always to see the other person's point of view. Liberalism seems to be a word that describes this state of mind, a word I always embraced, but perhaps did not fully understand.

At this stage, I feel it incumbent on me to point out, then try to explain why I have not used two words throughout this book. They are LOVE & HATE, both bandied about like confetti, used and misused, seemingly losing credibility, (at least in my mind), giving wrong messages to one and all. They have such multiple meanings, that surely there should be a multitude of new words invented to fill the void. The two words indicate to me an ultimate perfection, something total and unquestioning, which is why I try always to steer clear of them, believing there are usually degrees of feeling on most subjects, often without a word to describe them.

As I ponder a conclusion to this story, I feel a strong desire to keep the page open as I do for everyday living, for if we close doors, there is always the chance of locking out something you had not seen originally, to say nothing of the possibility of jamming your finger.

So I dive HEADLONG INTO LIFE from here on, with a final pledge to:

JUDGE NOBODY BUT MYSELF.

PEACE.

Acknowledgements

For their help in so many ways: Richard Lewis, Simon Hicks, Larry & Denise, Graham Lloyd, Peter & Caroline, Brenda & Alistair, Derick & Margaret, Robin Dyer, Peter Egan, Pat Davies, Christian Powell, Alison Payne, Ivor Alderson, Roger Warburton, and all Buddhist Thinkers.